THE PLEIADIAN STARSEED HANDBOOK

Understanding Your Role in the Galactic Family

Campbell Quinn McCarthy

S.D.N Publishing

Copyright © 2023 S.D.N Publishing

All rights reserved

The characters and events portrayed in this book are fictitious. Any similarity to real persons, living or dead, is coincidental and not intended by the author.

No part of this book may be reproduced, or stored in a retrieval system, or transmitted in any form or by any means, electronic, mechanical, photocopying, recording, or otherwise, without express written permission of the publisher.

ISBN: 9798866169405

CONTENTS

Title Page
Copyright
General Disclaimer   1
Introduction   4
Part I: Laying the Foundation   7
Chapter 1: What is a Starseed?   8
Chapter 2: An Overview of the Pleiadian Star System   12
Chapter 3: Galactic History: How Pleiadians Relate to Earth   15
Chapter 4: The Science Behind Starseeds: DNA and Soul Contracts   19
Chapter 5: The Different Types of Starseeds and Their Roles   23
Part II: Understanding Pleiadian Characteristics   27
Chapter 1: The Pleiadian Appearance   28
Chapter 2: The Emotional Landscape of Pleiadians   31
Chapter 3: Pleiadian Values and Ethics   34
Chapter 4: Social Dynamics Among Pleiadians   38
Chapter 5: How Pleiadians Communicate   41
Part III: Pleiadian Spirituality   45
Chapter 1: The Pleiadian View on Religion   46
Chapter 2: Pleiadian Healing Modalities   49
Chapter 3: Crystals and Energy Work: Pleiadian Tools   53

Chapter 4: The Pleiadian Perspective on Death and the Afterlife	57
Chapter 5: The Multidimensional Soul: Pleiadian Beliefs on Reincarnation	61
Part IV: Pleiadian Abilities and Gifts	65
Chapter 1: Telepathy: The Basics	66
Chapter 2: Empathy and Emotional Healing: Unlocking Your Potential	69
Chapter 3: Advanced Intuition: Trusting Your Gut	72
Chapter 4: Energy Manipulation and Healing	75
Chapter 5: Mastering Astral Projection	79
Part V: Your Connection to Pleiades	83
Chapter 1: Identifying Pleiadian Ancestry: Signs and Synchronicities	84
Chapter 2: Past Lives and Karmic Connections	88
Chapter 3: Dreams and Visions: Messages from Home	91
Chapter 4: The Akashic Records: Your Galactic History	94
Chapter 5: Developing a Stronger Connection: Practices and Techniques	98
Part VI: Meeting Other Starseeds	101
Chapter 1: Finding Your Soul Family	102
Chapter 2: The Importance of Community	105
Chapter 3: Navigating Relationships with Non-Starseeds	108
Chapter 4: Balancing Human Life with Galactic Commitments	111
Chapter 5: The Pleiadian Community on Earth	114
Part VII: Starseed Activations	118
Chapter 1: Activation Codes: What They Are and How to Use Them	119
Chapter 2: The Importance of Solar and Lunar Events	123

Chapter 3: Starseed Symbols and Sigils: Unlocking Your Gifts	126
Chapter 4: Activation Meditations	130
Chapter 5: Light Language: The Galactic Tongue	134
Part VIII: Challenges and Healing	138
Chapter 1: Earthly Struggles: Adjusting to 3D Life	139
Chapter 2: Emotional Blockages and How to Heal Them	143
Chapter 3: The Role of Ego: Lessons and Learning	147
Chapter 4: Balancing Dual Identities	150
Chapter 5: Building Resilience: Strategies for Difficult Times	154
Part IX: Working with Spirit Guides	158
Chapter 1: Who Are Spirit Guides?	159
Chapter 2: Contacting Your Pleiadian Guides	162
Chapter 3: Channeling Messages	165
Chapter 4: Enhancing Your Psychic Abilities	169
Chapter 5: Sacred Sites: Earthly Connections to Pleiadian Energies	173
Part X: Pleiadian Wisdom for Earthly Life	177
Chapter 1: Sustainable Living: A Pleiadian Approach	178
Chapter 2: Pleiadian Wisdom on Love and Relationships	181
Chapter 3: Career and Life Purpose: Aligning with Your Galactic Mission	184
Chapter 4: Pleiadian Practices for Emotional Well-Being	187
Chapter 5: Navigating Earthly Systems: Politics, Economics, and Social Structures	190
Part XI: Ethics and Responsibilities	193
Chapter 1: Free Will and Predestination	194
Chapter 2: Pleiadian Ethics on Healing and Manipulating	197

Energies

Chapter 3: The Universal Law of One	200
Chapter 4: The Galactic Federation: Structure and Governance	203
Chapter 5: Starseed Ethics in Human Society	207
Part XII: Upcoming Galactic Events	210
Chapter 1: The Great Awakening: What to Expect	211
Chapter 2: The Ascension Process: How It Affects You	214
Chapter 3: Cosmic Cycles and Their Influence	218
Chapter 4: Earth Changes: Pleiadian Perspectives	222
Chapter 5: Preparing for Contact: Practical Steps	225
Part XIII: Pleiadian Tools and Technologies	228
Chapter 1: Advanced Pleiadian Healing Instruments	229
Chapter 2: Starships and Interstellar Travel	232
Chapter 3: Pleiadian Architecture: Temples and Constructions	236
Chapter 4: The Pleiadian Relationship with AI	240
Chapter 5: Light Technology: Healing and Transformation	244
Part XIV: Your Mission on Earth	248
Chapter 1: Identifying Your Galactic Mission	249
Chapter 2: Aligning with Your Higher Self	252
Chapter 3: Practices for Spiritual Ascension	256
Chapter 4: Becoming a Lightworker or Wayshower	259
Chapter 5: Making an Impact: Humanitarian Work and Social Change	263
Part XV: The Road Ahead	266
Chapter 1: Prophecies and Predictions: The Pleiadian Outlook	267

Chapter 2: Developing a 5D Consciousness	271
Chapter 3: How to Prepare for the Future: Pleiadian Tips	275
Chapter 4: Creating Galactic Communities on Earth	278
Chapter 5: The Ongoing Journey: Your Evolving Role in the Galactic Family	282
Conclusion: An Uplifting Farewell: Continuing Your Cosmic Journey	285
THE END	289

GENERAL DISCLAIMER

This book is intended to provide informative and educational material on the subject matter covered. The author(s), publisher, and any affiliated parties make no representations or warranties with respect to the accuracy, applicability, completeness, or suitability of the contents herein and specifically disclaim any implied warranties of merchantability or fitness for a particular purpose.

The information contained in this book is for general information purposes only and is not intended to serve as legal, medical, financial, or any other form of professional advice. Readers should consult with appropriate professionals before making any decisions based on the information provided. Neither the author(s) nor the publisher shall be held responsible or liable for any loss, damage, injury, claim, or otherwise, whether direct or indirect, consequential, or incidental, that may occur as a result of applying or misinterpreting the information in this book.

This book may contain references to third-party websites, products, or services. Such references do not constitute an endorsement or recommendation, and the author(s) and publisher are not responsible for any outcomes related to these third-party references.

In no event shall the author(s), publisher, or any affiliated parties be liable for any direct, indirect, punitive, special, incidental, or other consequential damages arising directly or indirectly from any use of this material, which is provided "as is," and without warranties of any kind, express or implied.

By reading this book, you acknowledge and agree that you assume all risks and responsibilities concerning the applicability and consequences of the information provided. You also agree to indemnify, defend, and hold harmless the author(s), publisher, and any affiliated parties from any and all liabilities, claims, demands, actions, and causes of action whatsoever, whether or not foreseeable, that may arise from using or misusing the information contained in this book.

Although every effort has been made to ensure the accuracy of the information in this book as of the date of publication, the landscape of the subject matter covered is continuously evolving. Therefore, the author(s) and publisher expressly disclaim responsibility for any errors or omissions and reserve the right to update, alter, or revise the content without prior notice.

By continuing to read this book, you agree to be bound by the terms and conditions stated in this disclaimer. If you do not agree with these terms, it is your responsibility to discontinue use of this book immediately.

INTRODUCTION

A Warm Welcome to Your Galactic Family - The Path to Self-Discovery

Greetings and welcome, dear Starseeds and cosmic voyagers. You have embarked upon a journey that promises to be not just enlightening but also transformative. Whether you've always felt a mystical pull toward the cosmos, or you've recently stumbled upon the term "Starseed," this handbook is designed to be your guiding star. We will journey through the Pleiadian constellation, not as abstract celestial bodies but as part of a tangible, interconnected family—a Galactic Family, if you will.

The Core Purpose of This Handbook

While the universe is vast and its mysteries are abundant, the purpose of this handbook is sharply focused. This is a comprehensive guide to help you understand your unique role as a Pleiadian Starseed and how that fits into the broader tapestry of galactic life and energies. It serves to inform, to elucidate, and to resonate deeply with your inner knowing. We will dig into the Pleiadian belief systems, your psychic abilities, your ethical responsibilities, and even what the Pleiadian take is on earthly life. This book aims to be an encyclopedic reservoir of information, practices, and wisdom that will serve you well as you navigate your Earthly existence with Pleiadian consciousness.

A Sense of Cosmic Belonging

You might have often felt out of place, as if you don't quite fit into the societal norms and frameworks that surround you. This could be an indicator of your Starseed origin—a celestial lineage that transcends earthly bounds. As you navigate through this guide, it is our hope that you'll find resonance and validation, perhaps igniting dormant parts of your DNA or awakening latent abilities. You're not alone, and as you'll see, your being is part of a much greater cosmic design.

In the chapters that follow, you'll find sections carefully organized to walk you through various aspects of Pleiadian life, belief systems, and your role among them. The first part, "Laying the Foundation," will establish the basic framework for understanding what a Starseed is and how the Pleiadians fit into the larger galactic history. We'll delve into the science behind Starseeds, examining how DNA and soul contracts may be the physical and spiritual underpinnings of your cosmic identity.

Following that, we explore the characteristics that make Pleiadians unique—from their emotional spectrum to their intricate systems of communication. As we venture deeper, we'll cover the nuances of Pleiadian spirituality, a tapestry rich in beliefs about the multidimensional soul, reincarnation, and spiritual healing.

Your natural abilities and gifts are not to be left behind; a whole section is dedicated to understanding and nurturing your inherent psychic talents. We'll also focus on the actionable steps you can take to identify and strengthen your connection to the Pleiadian star system. Whether it's finding your soul family or grappling with the challenges of earthly life, each chapter aims to guide you with the wisdom and compassion that's characteristic of Pleiadian ethos.

Towards the end, we'll prepare you for what's ahead: upcoming galactic events that could shape your path, your ethical responsibilities, and ultimately, the grander mission you have on this Earth.

So, if you're ready to embark on this intricate journey of self-discovery and cosmic exploration, let's turn the page and start this adventure together. After all, in the grand tapestry of the cosmos, each one of us is a vital stitch. Welcome to your Galactic Family.

PART I: LAYING THE FOUNDATION

CHAPTER 1: WHAT IS A STARSEED?

Introduction

As you embark on your journey through the vast and wondrous landscape of Pleiadian wisdom and Starseed knowledge, it is crucial to start with a foundational understanding of what a Starseed actually is. This chapter aims to introduce you to the concept of Starseeds, their origin, purpose, and how they relate to the Pleiadian star system.

The Basic Concept of a Starseed

A Starseed is essentially a human being with a soul that originates from another star system, galaxy, or even another universe. While their physical bodies are entirely human, their spiritual essence is woven from a different celestial fabric. They are born into human families and live human lives, but deep down, there is a yearning for "home" that seems to come from somewhere far beyond the earthly realm. This sense of not quite belonging is often a hallmark trait of a Starseed, and it can be both a blessing and a challenge as they navigate life on Earth.

Starseeds and the Human Experience

Despite their cosmic origins, Starseeds are fully immersed in the human experience, complete with all its trials, tribulations, and joys. Many of them come to Earth with a sense of mission or purpose, which often revolves around helping humanity in some way. They may be driven to tackle social justice issues, push the boundaries of spirituality, or advance scientific understanding. Their unique perspective often makes them natural pioneers, healers, and leaders.

The Pleiadian Connection

In the context of this book, we focus on Pleiadian Starseeds, individuals whose souls are intricately linked with the Pleiadian star system, a cluster of stars located in the constellation of Taurus. Pleiadian Starseeds often exhibit traits that are characteristic of the Pleiadian ethos—values of compassion, unity, and spiritual advancement. These individuals often feel a particular affinity for Pleiadian wisdom and are drawn to the teaching and healing arts.

The Multidimensional Nature of Starseeds

Starseeds are multidimensional beings, which means that they exist across various dimensions of reality simultaneously. This multidimensionality is often experienced as an expansive sense of consciousness and may include psychic or paranormal abilities. For Pleiadian Starseeds, their multidimensional aspects often encompass the wisdom and experiences they have gathered from lifetimes in the Pleiadian system. This can manifest as intuitive knowledge, empathic abilities, or even vivid dreams and memories of other lifetimes.

Soul Contracts and Earthly Missions

Before incarnating on Earth, Starseeds often make what are

known as "soul contracts," agreements made on a soul level to fulfill specific missions or lessons during their earthly lifetime. These contracts can range from personal growth and healing to broader collective endeavors like societal change or environmental stewardship.

Unfolding Your Starseed Identity

Identifying as a Starseed is less about fitting into a specific mold and more about recognizing the unique blend of earthly and celestial characteristics that make up your individual identity. By embracing your Starseed origins, you can unlock a rich tapestry of experiences, abilities, and wisdom that can enrich not only your life but also the lives of those around you. As you navigate this earthly existence, it's essential to remember that being a Starseed is not an escape from human life but rather a deepening of it, adding layers of meaning, purpose, and connection to the broader universe.

Awakening to Your Starseed Nature

The process of awakening to one's Starseed identity can vary widely from person to person. Some may experience profound spiritual epiphanies, while others may undergo a more gradual unfolding. There are various ways to explore and confirm your Starseed heritage, including intuitive readings, meditation, and spiritual practices designed to connect you to your higher self and cosmic origins.

Summary

Understanding what a Starseed is forms the bedrock upon which the rest of your galactic journey rests. As multidimensional beings with earthly bodies and cosmic souls, Starseeds offer a unique blend of human experience and celestial wisdom. Specifically, Pleiadian Starseeds are closely aligned with values of compassion, unity, and spiritual growth. They often come to Earth with specific missions, guided by soul contracts made before their incarnation. Recognizing and embracing your Starseed nature is a journey unto itself, a transformative process that promises to deepen your experience of both earthly and cosmic existence.

CHAPTER 2: AN OVERVIEW OF THE PLEIADIAN STAR SYSTEM

In our quest to explore the mysteries and implications of being a Pleiadian Starseed, it becomes essential to delve into the celestial cradle that has given rise to such extraordinary beings—the Pleiadian star system. Commonly referred to as the "Seven Sisters," this star cluster is part of the Taurus constellation and is approximately 444 light-years away from Earth. In this chapter, we shall explore the key aspects of this cosmic sanctuary, focusing on its principal stars, intrinsic characteristics, and the philosophical import of its location and formation.

Principal Stars of Pleiades

While the Pleiadian star cluster contains numerous stars and celestial objects, seven bright stars serve as its cornerstone—namely Maia, Electra, Alcyone, Taygete, Celaeno, Sterope, and Merope. Each star is considered to possess unique energies and properties that resonate at different vibrational frequencies. These frequencies, in turn, are thought to influence the Pleiadian beings and, consequently, the Starseeds who find their origin here.

Alcyone, often called the "Central Sun," holds a particularly revered place, being the brightest star in the cluster and serving as a focal point for Pleiadian life. It is believed that Alcyone radiates profound spiritual energy, facilitating higher states of consciousness. The indigenous civilizations from these stars are said to be advanced, both technologically and spiritually, and harbor a deep sense of responsibility for cosmic evolution.

Characteristics: Spiritual and Material Abundance

The Pleiadian system is rich in spiritual and material resources. Although we don't possess concrete scientific evidence to map the exact topology of these distant worlds, various channels and intuitive sources describe Pleiadian planets as paradisiacal. Lush landscapes, crystalline waters, and harmonious coexistence of diverse ecosystems are some of the recurring themes in these accounts.

The Pleiadian way of life is often depicted as an ideal blend of technological advancement and deep-rooted spirituality. Their societies are organized around principles of equitable distribution of resources, unconditional love, and collective growth. The advancement in their technologies serves the higher purpose of spiritual ascension and cosmic equilibrium, making their civilization a beacon of holistic prosperity.

The Galactic Context: The Pleiades within the Milky Way

The Pleiadian system's position within the Milky Way galaxy holds symbolic and strategic importance. Often regarded as one of the galaxy's spiritual centers, Pleiades serves as a conduit for higher-dimensional energies to flow into our 3D reality. This makes the Pleiadian Starseeds important emissaries of light, facilitating the transfer of these energies to Earth for its collective evolution.

Moreover, Pleiades is part of a broader interstellar network that cooperates for the harmonious development of the galaxy. This network, sometimes referred to as the Galactic Federation, includes multiple advanced civilizations that have transcended the limitations of 3D existence and are committed to the upliftment of consciousness across the galaxy. Pleiadians, in this context, are highly respected for their spiritual wisdom and their ability to manifest peace and unity.

Summary

Understanding the Pleiadian star system is akin to decoding a cosmic blueprint that has immense implications for Starseeds and, by extension, for humanity. The system's principal stars, each with their unique vibrational frequencies, serve as both spiritual archetypes and sources of profound energy. Coupled with their abundant resources and advanced civilization, the Pleiades stands as a microcosm of cosmic harmony and spiritual enlightenment.

The Pleiadian system's location in the galaxy serves as a pivotal point for channeling higher-dimensional energies, contributing to the overall spiritual ecology of the Milky Way. By diving deep into the Pleiadian star system, we open new pathways for understanding our roles, our origins, and our destinies in this expansive cosmic drama.

CHAPTER 3: GALACTIC HISTORY: HOW PLEIADIANS RELATE TO EARTH

Introduction

In this chapter, we will delve into the fascinating interconnections between Pleiadians and Earth through a historical lens. Understanding the broader context of the Galactic Family can not only deepen your own self-awareness as a Pleiadian Starseed but also broaden your understanding of the intricate relationships that bind celestial bodies and civilizations. The chapter will cover the early Pleiadian involvement with Earth, their role in our planet's development, and how this historical perspective can illuminate your own role in the grand scheme.

The Ancient Pleiadian-Earth Connection

Long before the dawn of what we consider "modern civilization," Pleiadians had already established a symbiotic relationship with Earth. In Pleiadian cosmology, Earth is often referred to as a "sister planet," a title that underscores the depth and significance of the relationship. Pleiadians, with their advanced technology and spiritual wisdom, assisted early Earth civilizations in various ways, from transferring knowledge in the fields of agriculture and architecture to sharing insights into the workings of the cosmos. According to some records found in ancient texts—though altered and reinterpreted through the lens of Earthly civilizations—certain gods or deities worshipped by indigenous people were, in fact, Pleiadians who had visited the planet.

Why would a civilization as advanced as the Pleiadians involve themselves in Earthly matters? The answer lies in a concept known as "Galactic Stewardship." Pleiadians view the nurturing of less advanced civilizations as a sacred duty, one that brings both karmic balance and spiritual evolution to the galaxy at large. It's a mutual relationship that benefits both parties; while Earth civilizations received invaluable knowledge and wisdom, the Pleiadians gained a deeper understanding of physical existence and duality, enriching their own spiritual evolution.

Planetary Grids and Energy Ley Lines

Another aspect of the Pleiadian influence on Earth lies in the more subtle realms of energy and vibrational frequencies. The Pleiadians are said to have been involved in the activation and maintenance of Earth's "energy grids," sometimes referred to as ley lines. These are invisible lines of force that crisscross the planet and act as conduits for subtle energies. Ancient Earth monuments such as the pyramids of Giza, Stonehenge, and many others are believed to be built upon these ley lines. The Pleiadian influence is not just in the creation of these energy grids, but also in the activation of certain energy points, akin to acupressure on a cosmic scale. This helps in the elevation of Earth's collective consciousness and serves as a balancing act against denser, lower vibrations.

Understanding this ancient, yet active, relationship with Earth's energy grids can be empowering for a Pleiadian Starseed. It might offer clarity on why certain locations on Earth feel energetically potent and why you might be instinctually drawn to participate in activities that involve healing the planet, be it environmental activism, or energy work aimed at raising collective human consciousness.

The Future of Pleiadian Involvement

The relationship between Pleiadians and Earth is not a relic of the past; it continues to evolve. The current epoch is viewed by many Pleiadian Starseeds as a critical juncture in Earth's history. Our planet is undergoing a shift in consciousness, sometimes referred to as the "Great Awakening." During this transformative period, the Pleiadian involvement is believed to intensify, with many Starseeds incarnating on Earth to assist in this global transformation. As a Pleiadian Starseed, understanding the galactic history may offer you greater clarity and purpose in navigating the complex landscape of Earthly existence at this pivotal time. You are not just a bystander but an active participant in a cosmic play of unimaginable scale.

Summary

In sum, the Pleiadian-Earth relationship is multifaceted, deeply rooted in history, and continuously evolving. From sharing advanced knowledge with early civilizations to their ongoing influence in Earth's energetic makeup, the Pleiadians have been inextricably tied to the story of our planet. For a Pleiadian Starseed, understanding this rich history provides not just a backdrop but a living tapestry that informs your purpose and role in the Galactic Family. As Earth ventures further into a crucial period of transformation, the Pleiadian relationship with this planet is likely to continue evolving, offering new opportunities for engagement, growth, and cosmic co-creation.

CHAPTER 4: THE SCIENCE BEHIND STARSEEDS: DNA AND SOUL CONTRACTS

Introduction

In this chapter, we delve into the scientific theories that are often discussed in the context of Starseeds and particularly Pleiadian Starseeds. Two key components form the basis of these theories: DNA activation and soul contracts. Although these terms are frequently cited in spiritual and New Age discussions, they also carry weight in certain scientific dialogues. By understanding these elements, you will gain a more nuanced view of what it means to be a Pleiadian Starseed and how you might be connected to the broader Galactic Family.

The DNA Activation Theory

One of the most discussed theories within the Starseed community is the notion of DNA activation. According to this theory, all living beings, including humans, possess latent strands of DNA that remain "deactivated" in a typical 3D Earth experience. These dormant strands, often referred to as "junk DNA" in conventional scientific parlance, are believed to hold abilities, memories, and traits from past lives and other dimensions.

In the case of Pleiadian Starseeds, this DNA activation allows for a stronger connection to be formed with the Pleiadian star system, including the assimilation of Pleiadian traits and abilities. Some advocates of this theory propose that the activation occurs naturally over time through spiritual growth and self-awareness. Others suggest that specific activation techniques can catalyze this process, including meditation, energy work, and certain vibrational sounds or symbols.

When the "junk DNA" becomes activated, it purportedly enables access to higher states of consciousness, more profound spiritual experiences, and even psychic abilities. In the broader scientific community, the idea of "junk DNA" having latent functions is being explored, although no definitive conclusions have been reached. Still, the notion aligns interestingly with the spiritual perspectives on DNA activation in the context of Starseeds.

Soul Contracts and Their Role

Soul contracts are another fundamental concept that intertwines with the experience of being a Pleiadian Starseed. While the term isn't standard in mainstream science, the concept has roots in various spiritual and philosophical traditions. A soul contract is essentially an agreement made between souls before incarnating into the physical world. These contracts outline specific lessons to be learned, relationships to be encountered, and missions to be carried out during the lifetime.

For Pleiadian Starseeds, the soul contract often includes clauses related to awakening to their Pleiadian heritage, fulfilling certain roles within the Earthly realm, and aiding in the global or even galactic ascension process. These contracts are not set in stone but serve as a framework or roadmap for the soul's journey. Understanding your soul contract can provide greater insight into your life's purpose, challenges, and relationships. Some Starseeds use methods like past-life regressions, Akashic Record readings, or intuitive guidance to gain a clearer understanding of their soul contracts.

Bridging Science and Spirituality

The theories of DNA activation and soul contracts sit at an intriguing intersection between science and spirituality. While not fully supported or explained by current scientific paradigms, these concepts are increasingly drawing attention from researchers interested in the frontiers of consciousness and human potential. For instance, the study of epigenetics is beginning to explore how environmental factors, including emotional and mental states, can impact DNA expression. Similarly, the field of quantum physics is probing the very nature of reality, consciousness, and the interconnectedness of all things, offering some scientific backbone to spiritual ideas.

As science advances, it's likely that more connections will be made, allowing for a more comprehensive understanding of these complex theories. Until then, they remain powerful frameworks for understanding the unique experiences and abilities of Pleiadian Starseeds.

Summary

In this chapter, we have explored two foundational theories that many in the Starseed community find invaluable for understanding their role and abilities. DNA activation touches on the scientific mystery of "junk DNA" and how its activation may unlock hidden potentials and connections to other realms. Soul contracts offer a more metaphysical perspective, proposing that our lives are guided by pre-existing agreements that delineate our paths and purposes. Both of these ideas sit at the crossroads of science and spirituality, a place where increasingly more researchers are turning their attention. Understanding these theories can offer you not just solace but also actionable insights into your life journey as a Pleiadian Starseed.

CHAPTER 5: THE DIFFERENT TYPES OF STARSEEDS AND THEIR ROLES

Introduction

Having explored what it means to be a Starseed, delved into the Pleiadian star system, and touched on the science behind Starseeds, it's now time to explore the diverse spectrum of Starseeds and their respective roles. Understanding the types of Starseeds and their unique characteristics can offer a richer, more nuanced perspective on your place within the Galactic Family. This chapter aims to provide a brief look at some of the major types of Starseeds and how their roles manifest on Earth and within the wider cosmic context.

Pleiadian Starseeds

Pleiadian Starseeds often resonate with the traits of empathy, wisdom, and love for humanity. They are drawn to healing arts and often become wayshowers, lightworkers, or spiritual mentors. Their roles are often to assist in the ascension of Earth by uplifting human consciousness and aiding in the healing of the planet on both an ecological and spiritual level. They also frequently act as bridges between dimensions, being adept at navigating the physical and spiritual realms.

Sub-Types of Pleiadian Starseeds

1. **Maian Starseeds**: Originating from the star Maia in the Pleiadian star cluster, these Starseeds are often involved in leadership roles, whether it be in community organizations or spiritual movements.
2. **Electran Starseeds**: From the star Electra, these Starseeds are known for their passion for justice and balance. They often find themselves in roles advocating for fairness and equality.
3. **Taygetan Starseeds**: Originating from Taygeta, these Starseeds are deeply intuitive and are often involved in the psychic arts or energy healing fields.

Sirian Starseeds

Sirian Starseeds are from the star system Sirius, the brightest star in our night sky. Often highly intellectual, they are frequently attracted to science and technology. They possess a unique ability to analyze complex systems, making them excellent problem solvers. Sirians are often focused on social justice issues, sustainability, and restructuring societal systems that are in disrepair.

Sub-Types of Sirian Starseeds

1. **Sirian A Starseeds**: They lean more towards the intellectual and technological side, often drawn to careers in engineering, information technology, or theoretical sciences.

2. **Sirian B Starseeds**: More spiritually inclined, these individuals are interested in mysticism, spiritual enlightenment, and ascension.

Andromedan Starseeds

Hailing from the Andromeda galaxy, Andromedan Starseeds are known for their independent nature and strong drive for personal freedom. They often have difficulties adapting to societal norms and may live unconventional lifestyles. Their role is often to challenge the status quo and offer alternative ways of thinking and living, thus sparking societal evolution.

Sub-Types of Andromedan Starseeds

1. **Cerebral Andromedans**: These are the thinkers and philosophers, always questing for truth and wisdom.
2. **Mystical Andromedans**: These individuals are more focused on spiritual evolution and often engage in metaphysical practices, exploring the boundaries of human consciousness.

The Overarching Role of Starseeds

Starseeds, irrespective of their origin, generally serve as catalysts for change, enlightenment, and healing on Earth. They are often placed in challenging life circumstances that enable them to forge a unique path, providing them with the experiences needed to fulfill their roles effectively. Starseeds are incarnated in human form but carry with them the energy and wisdom of their star families. By walking among us, they help to raise the collective vibration of humanity, guiding us toward a future of higher consciousness and spiritual awareness.

Conclusion

Understanding the types of Starseeds and their respective roles can significantly deepen your understanding of your place in the broader cosmic picture. Whether you are a Pleiadian focused on healing and spiritual guidance, a Sirian oriented towards intellectual pursuits and social justice, or an Andromedan pushing the boundaries of conventional thought, recognizing your type and role can be enlightening. This acknowledgment not only enriches your personal journey but also contributes to your ability to fulfill your galactic mission effectively.

PART II: UNDERSTANDING PLEIADIAN CHARACTERISTICS

CHAPTER 1: THE PLEIADIAN APPEARANCE

Introduction

In our journey to explore the intricacies of the Pleiadian Starseed experience, one facet that has often captivated people is the physical appearance of Pleiadians. Many theories and discussions have arisen around how Pleiadians look, why they look that way, and what that means for their interaction with Earth and its inhabitants. In this chapter, we will delve into the commonly held perspectives on Pleiadian appearance and its broader implications.

Common Traits

Among the most frequently cited physical traits attributed to Pleiadians are their blue or blue-green eyes, fair or slightly golden-toned skin, and typically blond or light-colored hair. However, it's crucial to note that not all Pleiadians will fit this description. Pleiadian Starseeds incarnated on Earth may have a wide range of appearances, influenced by their earthly genetics. Yet, certain telltale signs can often resonate with their Pleiadian origins. For instance, a sense of magnetism or an ethereal aura are commonly noted. People often report feeling a sense of peace, or an inexplicable attraction toward Pleiadian Starseeds, sometimes without knowing why.

Moreover, Pleiadians are often thought to have a more youthful appearance, which doesn't seem to align with their actual age. Theories suggest that their higher vibrational frequency impacts not just their spiritual form but also their physical form, allowing them to age more gracefully.

Energetic Resonance

While physical appearance provides a way to identify Pleiadian characteristics superficially, the most defining aspect is said to be their energetic resonance. Pleiadians, like other higher-dimensional beings, are made up of a more refined and higher frequency energy. This can manifest as a certain luminosity, an almost glowing skin, or an aura that many sensitive individuals can perceive.

Many people report an uplifting shift in their own energy fields when in the presence of a Pleiadian. This shift isn't just psychological; it often manifests as a physical sensation, like tingling in the skin or a sense of euphoria. It's as if the Pleiadian's energy field acts like a tuning fork, causing nearby frequencies to adjust and resonate at a higher level. In practical terms, this can result in heightened intuition, clarity of thought, and a general sense of well-being for those who come into contact with Pleiadians, whether they are aware of their otherworldly origins or not.

Evolutionary Context

The physical and energetic traits of Pleiadians are said to be closely tied to their evolutionary journey. Pleiadians are believed to have undergone significant evolutionary leaps in their distant past, allowing them to ascend into higher dimensional states.

As beings who are attuned to fifth-dimensional consciousness and above, their bodies and energy fields have adapted to these frequencies. This adaptability manifests in their appearance, both in the Pleiades star system and when they incarnate on Earth.

This higher frequency existence also impacts their biological functionality. Their bodies are often considered to be more finely tuned instruments of their consciousness, capable of quicker cellular regeneration and possessing a more efficient energy exchange system. This has implications not just for their longevity but also for their ability to manipulate energies, heal, and even their psychic capabilities, which we will explore in subsequent chapters.

Summary

In wrapping up this chapter, it's essential to remember that while appearances can offer clues about one's Pleiadian connections, they are by no means definitive proof. The real essence of a Pleiadian, or any Starseed, is captured in their energy, their frequency, and the resonance they create with the world around them. Physical features can indeed be intriguing and are often a point of curiosity, but the Pleiadian experience transcends the physical realm. It is an integrated experience, melding body, mind, and spirit in a dance of cosmic harmony that reflects their evolutionary history and higher dimensional existence. So, whether you identify as a Pleiadian Starseed or are simply curious about them, it's crucial to consider these characteristics as part of a larger, more complex tapestry of galactic heritage.

CHAPTER 2: THE EMOTIONAL LANDSCAPE OF PLEIADIANS

In the grand tapestry of the cosmos, Pleiadians stand out not just for their physical attributes or advanced technology, but for their emotional depth and complexity. This chapter delves into the emotional landscape that typifies a Pleiadian, from their approach to love and relationships to the way they handle challenges and conflict. Understanding these intricacies can offer valuable insights into your own emotional life, particularly if you identify as a Pleiadian Starseed.

The Primacy of Emotional Intelligence

In Pleiadian society, emotional intelligence is considered just as crucial, if not more so, than other forms of intelligence such as logical or spatial intelligence. From an early age, Pleiadians are taught to nurture their emotional well-being, and educational systems are designed to foster skills like empathy, self-awareness, and emotional regulation. The holistic approach to emotional growth enables Pleiadians to navigate complex social dynamics effectively, making them excellent mediators and diplomats. Their emotional acumen often facilitates advanced forms of communication, including telepathy, which we will explore in later chapters.

This focus on emotional intelligence has a historical context. Pleiadian civilizations have undergone periods of significant upheaval and transformation. Overcoming these challenges has required not just technological solutions but a deeply ingrained sense of emotional resilience and community spirit. As a result, emotional intelligence is woven into the fabric of Pleiadian culture, guiding both their interpersonal interactions and their broader philosophical outlook.

Emotional Traits: Sensitivity, Empathy, and Compassion

Pleiadians are often described as deeply sensitive beings, highly attuned to the emotions of others. This sensitivity serves as both a gift and a challenge. On the one hand, it allows Pleiadians to form deep and meaningful relationships easily. Their empathy often extends beyond their immediate social circles, influencing their interactions with other species and civilizations. This emotional sensitivity often manifests in a heightened sense of compassion, a trait that has led Pleiadians to engage in various humanitarian efforts across galaxies.

However, this intense sensitivity can also be a double-edged sword. Pleiadians are vulnerable to feeling overwhelmed, especially when exposed to environments with harsh emotional climates. They often require periods of solitude or tranquility to recharge and regain emotional equilibrium. Failing to recognize and respect this need can lead to emotional burnout, a state that can have significant repercussions given the centrality of emotional well-being in Pleiadian life.

Relationships and Emotional Bonds

Love and relationships occupy a special place in Pleiadian

life. Unlike many other civilizations where relationships may be constrained by social norms or traditions, Pleiadians have a more fluid and expansive view of love. Relationships are considered sacred contracts, formed not just for procreation or social stability but for mutual spiritual and emotional growth. Therefore, it's common for Pleiadians to form partnerships based on a deep sense of spiritual connection rather than merely physical or intellectual attraction.

Moreover, the Pleiadian approach to relationships often transcends the limitations of time and space. They believe in the concept of soul families or groups of souls that incarnate together over multiple lifetimes to fulfill a shared mission. Thus, the emotional bonds formed are viewed as eternal, enduring across lifetimes and dimensions. This outlook instills relationships with a profound sense of purpose and depth, making them a cornerstone of Pleiadian emotional life.

Summary

Pleiadians are emotionally rich beings, valuing emotional intelligence as a critical aspect of their civilization. Their emotional traits include a high degree of sensitivity, empathy, and compassion, which enable them to form meaningful relationships but also pose challenges requiring mindful self-care. In Pleiadian culture, relationships are not mere social constructs but spiritual contracts, formed for mutual growth and bound by a sense of eternal connection. Understanding the emotional landscape of Pleiadians can offer invaluable insights into your own emotional world, especially if you identify as a Pleiadian Starseed.

CHAPTER 3: PLEIADIAN VALUES AND ETHICS

Introduction

Welcome to the third chapter of Part II, focusing on Pleiadian values and ethics. By understanding these, you can delve deeper into your galactic heritage and strengthen your connection with the Pleiadian energies that may be influencing your life. Exploring the ethical framework and cultural norms of the Pleiadians will provide you with a broader understanding of how these characteristics manifest in your earthly life. Let's delve into the core values, ethical systems, and cultural perspectives that define the Pleiadian way of being.

Core Values: The Pillars of Pleiadian Society

The Pleiadians, as part of their galactic heritage, have developed a unique set of core values that differ considerably from what is commonly found on Earth. These values are often categorized into three main pillars:

1. **Unity Consciousness**: Pleiadians operate on the belief that all life is interconnected. This manifests as a strong sense of community and an aversion to actions that promote separation or disunity. The focus is on

collective well-being, often leading to societal systems that prioritize shared resources and egalitarianism.

2. **Sovereignty of Being**: Pleiadians are firm advocates of individual freedom and the sovereignty of one's own existence. Despite the emphasis on collective unity, they believe that individuality is a sacred facet of the whole. Self-expression and authenticity are highly regarded, as they contribute to the intricate tapestry of Pleiadian society.

3. **Harmony with Nature**: Living in equilibrium with their environment is another cornerstone of Pleiadian ethics. They believe that nature is a conscious entity with which one must establish a symbiotic relationship. Sustainability and ecological balance are not just political issues for Pleiadians but are deeply rooted in their spiritual worldview.

Ethical Systems: Moral Codification

Understanding the core values of Pleiadian society can provide a framework for grasping their ethical system, which is both complex and intuitive. A blend of consequentialism and virtue ethics seems to dominate their moral landscape.

1. **Consequentialism**: Pleiadians evaluate the moral implications of an action based on its effects. Unlike some Earthly philosophical standpoints that focus solely on intent or inherent goodness, Pleiadians consider the ripples an action will send throughout the community and beyond. This often leads to a more holistic form of decision-making, wherein the good of the collective is weighed against individual needs or wants.

2. **Virtue Ethics**: While they do consider consequences, Pleiadians also place great emphasis on the virtues

exhibited by individuals. Virtue ethics in Pleiadian society can be compared to the classical Earthly concept, where traits like wisdom, courage, and compassion are not just personal attributes but communal responsibilities. Individuals strive to embody these virtues, as they contribute to the collective harmony and well-being of their society.

Cultural Perspectives: The Pleiadian Outlook on Earthly Issues

Many Starseeds find themselves at odds with Earth's mainstream perspectives on various issues, from politics to spirituality. This often stems from their inherent Pleiadian values and ethical systems that stand in stark contrast to Earthly norms.

For example, the Pleiadian viewpoint on justice involves restorative practices that focus on healing for all parties involved rather than punitive measures. They also approach subjects like wealth and power very differently, often shunning the idea of accumulating resources for individual gain. Instead, resources are viewed as communal assets that should be distributed in a way that benefits the entire society.

Similarly, their outlook on relationships is geared more towards soul connections rather than superficial or materialistic bonds. This could manifest in Starseeds as a yearning for deeper emotional connections and a sense of disillusionment with Earth's often transactional approach to relationships.

Conclusion

Understanding the Pleiadian values and ethical systems can offer profound insights into why you may feel the way you do, especially if you identify as a Pleiadian Starseed. This chapter aimed to elucidate the core values, ethical landscape, and cultural perspectives that shape Pleiadian society. Gaining a deeper understanding of these can help you better navigate your earthly life while honoring your galactic heritage. As you move forward, consider how these values resonate with your own beliefs and how they could be integrated into your daily life for a more harmonious existence.

CHAPTER 4: SOCIAL DYNAMICS AMONG PLEIADIANS

In the pursuit of understanding Pleiadian characteristics more comprehensively, it's crucial to delve into the social structures and relations that shape Pleiadian societies. Pleiadian cultures, while diverse across various planets and star systems within the Pleiadian constellation, share some underlying principles when it comes to social dynamics. This chapter aims to explore these dynamics, providing valuable insights into group behaviors, leadership styles, and the concept of community among Pleiadians.

Group Behavior and Interpersonal Relationships

Pleiadians put a high emphasis on cooperative behavior and mutual respect within any group setting. Whether it's a family, a work team, or a spiritual circle, the core tenet remains the same: everyone's voice matters, and consensus is often sought in decision-making processes. There's a shared belief that collective wisdom surpasses individual knowledge. This results in environments where members are encouraged to share thoughts openly and respectfully listen to others.

Within these group dynamics, individual differences are not only tolerated but celebrated. Pleiadians believe that diversity enriches the collective experience and provides opportunities for growth and expansion. This belief system goes beyond mere platitudes; it's ingrained in their educational, religious, and governance structures. Therefore, it is not uncommon to find hybrid groups that combine various skills, backgrounds, and even species for the sake of achieving a common goal.

Leadership and Governance

When discussing leadership, Pleiadian societies often operate on principles of servant leadership rather than hierarchical authority. Leaders are seen as facilitators and guides rather than rulers, and they earn their positions through demonstrated wisdom, compassion, and competence, rather than through coercion or inheritance. Pleiadian leaders often have high emotional intelligence and are adept at conflict resolution, qualities which are rigorously cultivated from a young age.

The governance structures reflect this ethos, often resembling councils or collectives rather than rigid hierarchies. Such assemblies might include individuals from diverse fields and walks of life, from spiritual teachers to scientists, artists, and social workers. Decisions are generally made by collective agreement, and the concept of a veto power is either non-existent or highly restricted, highlighting once again the Pleiadian penchant for inclusive decision-making.

Community and Collective Consciousness

In Pleiadian culture, the concept of community extends beyond physical or geographical proximity. Due to their advanced empathic and telepathic abilities, Pleiadians experience what could be described as a form of collective consciousness. This heightened sense of interconnectedness serves as a powerful tool for rapid information exchange, problem-solving, and emotional support. While individuality is respected, the greater good of the community takes precedence in most aspects of life.

This collective consciousness is not to be misunderstood as a hive mind that overrides individual thought. Instead, it serves as an expanded network of awareness and empathy, allowing for a more nuanced understanding of each individual's needs and contributions. This can be especially useful in times of crisis or major decision-making, where the input and well-being of the many can be considered almost instantaneously.

In summary, social dynamics among Pleiadians are characterized by a focus on cooperative behavior, collective decision-making, and a deeply ingrained sense of community. Leadership is facilitative rather than authoritative, and the wellbeing of the community is often placed at the forefront of individual endeavors. This creates societies where diversity is celebrated, empathy is the norm, and collective wisdom is highly valued. Understanding these dynamics can provide valuable insights for Starseeds and others interested in Pleiadian culture, offering lessons that could be beneficial for Earth's own evolving social structures.

CHAPTER 5: HOW PLEIADIANS COMMUNICATE

Introduction

Communication is a cornerstone of any civilization, and for Pleiadians, the modes and methods of conveying messages are both diverse and complex. This chapter seeks to unpack the nuanced approaches Pleiadians use to communicate, both with each other and with beings from other dimensions or galaxies. From verbal communication and body language to telepathy and energetic resonance, understanding the methods of Pleiadian communication can enrich your understanding of your place in the Galactic Family.

Verbal and Non-Verbal Expressions

Pleiadians are known for their eloquence and artistic use of language. They frequently employ metaphors, analogies, and poetic structures to convey complex ideas in a digestible manner. Their spoken language is musical and tonal, filled with rhythmic patterns and harmonic vibrations that carry not just information but also emotional nuances.

Although many Pleiadians are fluent in various languages of the Universe, including a capacity for understanding human languages, they place a high value on non-verbal forms of communication as well. For example, eye contact among Pleiadians is a rich tapestry of information exchange. A simple gaze can convey an array of emotions, intentions, and even specific messages. Similarly, their body language, such as the posture or positioning of hands, can serve as subtle but effective forms of communication. Their movement is often synchronized and fluid, reflecting a collective coherence in thought and emotion.

Telepathic Connections

Telepathy is a fundamental form of communication among Pleiadians. For them, this is not a specialized skill but a natural way of life. Telepathic connections can be categorized into two broad types: individual telepathy and collective telepathic networks.

Individual Telepathy

In one-on-one interactions, Pleiadians use telepathy to convey not just words but also emotions, concepts, and vivid experiences. This form of communication is multi-layered and operates in what could be described as a "quantum realm" of interaction, where multiple streams of information can be transmitted and received simultaneously. This enables them to have highly nuanced and intricate conversations that go far beyond the limitations of verbal language.

Collective Telepathic Networks

On a larger scale, Pleiadians participate in what might be called telepathic "hubs" or "networks," allowing them to share information and emotional states across vast distances. These networks are not static but are dynamic systems that adapt and evolve. They can be likened to the human concept of the "collective unconscious," but in a more conscious, active form. Through these networks, Pleiadians maintain a sense of unity and collective identity, even when they are separated across different dimensions or planetary systems.

Energetic Resonance and Frequency Matching

In addition to the more straightforward methods of communication, Pleiadians also use energetic resonance as a means of non-verbal communication. Every being emits a unique energetic "signature" that can be felt by those who are sensitive to it. Pleiadians are particularly adept at reading these energies and can gauge the emotional state, intentions, and even the thought patterns of another being based on this energetic resonance.

This form of communication is not just passive; Pleiadians can actively modulate their energy to "match frequencies" with another being. This is often done in healing practices, teaching scenarios, or any interaction that requires deep empathy and understanding. When two beings match frequencies, the exchange of information becomes more seamless, encompassing not just words or thoughts, but entire experiences and wisdom.

Summary

Communication among Pleiadians is a multifaceted phenomenon that extends well beyond the limitations of spoken or written language. From the eloquence of their verbal expressions and the depth of their non-verbal cues to the intricacy of their telepathic connections and the nuance of energetic resonance, Pleiadian communication methods offer a rich tapestry of meaningful interaction. As you grow more attuned to your Pleiadian heritage, you may find that understanding and even adopting these forms of communication can offer profound insights into your relationships, both earthly and galactic, and deepen your connection to the Cosmic Family.

PART III: PLEIADIAN SPIRITUALITY

CHAPTER 1: THE PLEIADIAN VIEW ON RELIGION

Introduction

In your journey to better understand your place within the Galactic Family as a Pleiadian Starseed, delving into the realm of spirituality becomes crucial. The fabric of your soul, woven through the cosmos, is imbued with spiritual essence and potential. While human religions often draw from ancient texts, hierarchical structures, and cultural mores, Pleiadian spirituality takes a different approach. Understanding these nuances is essential for harmonizing your earthly experience with your galactic self.

Beyond Dogma: The Fluidity of Belief Systems

In Pleiadian culture, religion isn't confined to temples, books, or centralized organizations. Rather, it is an omnipresent life philosophy that permeates everyday activities, relationships, and even the Pleiadian approach to science and technology. This seamless integration sidesteps the dogmatic trappings that often accompany earthly religions.

One of the core tenets is the interconnectedness of all beings and things, a concept that is deeply ingrained in Pleiadian culture. Whether it is the dance of planets in their orbits or the symbiotic relationship between species on a given world, this underlying principle is considered sacred. In contrast to Earth's dualistic interpretations—good versus evil, divine versus mortal—Pleiadians understand existence through a lens of unity and diversity co-existing in a complex weave.

Cosmic Spirituality: A Galactic Perspective

In Pleiadian spirituality, the cosmos itself is considered a living, breathing entity, of which all beings are part. There is an inherent understanding that consciousness exists in many forms and dimensions, some incomprehensible to even the most advanced Pleiadian thinkers. This perspective instills a sense of humility and awe towards the universe, making spiritual exploration a natural inclination for Pleiadians. It also validates their understanding of reincarnation, astral travel, and multi-dimensional existence.

For Pleiadians, spirituality isn't merely a set of rituals or beliefs but an ongoing journey of discovery that can involve travel between different worlds, dimensions, and states of consciousness. The infinite possibilities of existence are explored with a sense of adventure and reverence, embracing the mystery that comes with it.

The Role of Intuition and Inner Wisdom

Unlike many Earth religions that place spiritual authority in the hands of a chosen few, Pleiadian spirituality encourages individuals to seek their own truths. Intuition is highly revered as a valuable form of wisdom that complements rational thought. Pleiadians often spend time in meditative or trance-like states to connect with their inner selves and the universal consciousness. They believe that each individual, by virtue of being a facet of the greater cosmic entity, carries within them a spark of divine wisdom.

This emphasis on individual spiritual journeys doesn't mean Pleiadians are isolated in their practices. On the contrary, they frequently gather to share insights, experiences, and to collectively tune into higher states of consciousness. These gatherings are not presided over by a singular spiritual leader but are collaborative, valuing the input and experience of each participant.

Summary

As a Pleiadian Starseed, your approach to spirituality is likely to be deeply influenced by these cosmic perspectives. Understanding the Pleiadian view on religion offers not just an insight into their culture but also provides alternative approaches to spiritual growth that can enrich your life on Earth. By valuing interconnectedness, embracing the cosmos as a living entity, and cherishing individual spiritual quests, you align yourself more closely with the Pleiadian ethos. It invites you to explore spirituality as a limitless journey, rather than a destination, as you continue to navigate your dual existence—both as a human and as a member of your wider Galactic Family.

CHAPTER 2: PLEIADIAN HEALING MODALITIES

Introduction

As we traverse the enlightening pathway of Pleiadian spirituality, it becomes necessary to explore the core healing modalities embraced by Pleiadians. These are not just physical methods of curing ailments; they are holistic approaches aimed at aligning the body, mind, and spirit with the universal energies. Let's delve into the unique Pleiadian healing methodologies, covering vibrational healing, energy harmonization, and the transcendental process of spiritual cleansing. These processes encapsulate the Pleiadian holistic vision of well-being that Starseeds can integrate into their earthly lives.

Vibrational Healing: The Frequency of Wholeness

Pleiadians understand that the universe is a complex symphony of vibrations. Everything in existence, from the smallest particle to the largest celestial body, resonates with specific frequencies. Illness or discord, whether mental, emotional, or physical, is seen as a distortion or disruption in these natural vibrations.

To realign and restore balance, Pleiadians employ vibrational healing methods that use sound, color, and geometric patterns. Sound baths with harmonically resonant instruments like crystal bowls, tuning forks, or even vocalizations are commonly utilized. By matching the frequencies of these sounds with that of the individual's energy field, healing and rejuvenation are facilitated.

Colors, often emanating from various light sources or visualizations, are also an integral part of this healing modality. Different hues correspond to specific energy centers or chakras in the body. For instance, blue light might be focused on the throat chakra to aid in communication, while green might be used to balance the heart chakra, fostering love and compassion.

Energy Harmonization: The Flow of Cosmic Forces

Another pillar in the Pleiadian healing arsenal is energy harmonization. This process involves the manipulation and direction of life force energy, often termed 'Chi,' 'Prana,' or in Pleiadian terminology, 'Vorin.' Vorin flows through everything and is the sustaining power that bridges the material and spiritual realms.

Pleiadian healers act as conduits for this energy, channeling it through their hands or even from a distance through intention and focus. Techniques resemble those found in earthly practices like Reiki or Qigong, but with a more refined understanding of cosmic geometries and celestial influences. They also incorporate the use of symbols, both mentally envisioned and physically drawn, to focus and amplify the energy work. For instance, a specific Pleiadian sigil may be visualized or drawn over a person's abdomen to aid in digestive issues or enhance personal power.

The energy work isn't limited to individual well-being. Pleiadians also direct Vorin for environmental healing, often in conjunction with crystals to amplify and sustain the positive energy flow. This aligns not just the individual but the collective and planetary vibrations as well.

Spiritual Cleansing: The Transcendental Elixir

Beyond the physical and energetic layers of existence lies the spiritual realm, and Pleiadians emphasize the importance of addressing issues rooted here through a process called Spiritual Cleansing. This involves a series of guided visualizations, meditations, and rituals aimed at shedding accumulated spiritual toxins and karmic baggage.

Using the spiritual technology of thought-forms and intention, participants are guided through symbolic scenarios that might involve purifying fires, transformative vortexes, or encounters with enlightened beings, often personalized to the individual's spiritual heritage and galactic lineage. This process not only purifies the individual but also realigns them with their higher self and cosmic mission, thus coming full circle to the Pleiadian view of holistic well-being.

Conclusion

Understanding Pleiadian healing modalities provides an enriching dimension to how we can approach well-being from a more holistic standpoint. Vibrational healing aligns us with the fundamental frequencies of the universe, energy harmonization manipulates the universal life force for targeted healing, and spiritual cleansing aids in the elimination of soul-level burdens and karmic debris. Integrating these profound practices into one's life can bring a fulfilling sense of balance, health, and alignment with both earthly and cosmic purposes. This knowledge serves as another vital step in comprehending your role and responsibilities as a Pleiadian Starseed in this grand cosmic tableau.

CHAPTER 3: CRYSTALS AND ENERGY WORK: PLEIADIAN TOOLS

Introduction

The spiritual toolbox of a Pleiadian Starseed often consists of more than just abstract concepts and ethereal practices. Physical elements such as crystals and specific energy work techniques play a significant role in amplifying and fine-tuning the vibrational frequencies that facilitate the Starseed's multidimensional functions. This chapter seeks to illuminate the intricate relationship between Pleiadian spirituality and the material tools that serve as conduits for energy manipulation, spiritual growth, and consciousness expansion.

The Resonance of Crystals in Pleiadian Practices

Crystals, in Pleiadian spirituality, are more than just ornamental or decorative. They are meticulously chosen instruments that hold specific vibrational frequencies and characteristics. The Pleiadians assert that crystals contain a form of consciousness derived from their mineral components, originating from the celestial bodies on which they were formed. Different crystals possess energies corresponding to particular needs and cosmic frequencies, serving to both amplify and modulate energy.

Many Pleiadian Starseeds already feel a natural inclination towards certain crystals, instinctively choosing those that resonate with their energetic needs. Quartz crystals, for example, are common Pleiadian tools due to their versatility and amplification properties. Amethyst, with its calming energies and connection to spiritual wisdom, is often employed for meditation and intuitive practices. Moldavite is another fascinating example; this green, scaly-textured stone is believed to possess interdimensional energies that resonate closely with Pleiadian frequencies.

Pleiadian Techniques in Energy Work

Energy work constitutes a core practice within Pleiadian spirituality. While the idea of manipulating energy might sound abstract or nebulous, Pleiadians provide systematic methods designed to facilitate flow, remove blockages, and elevate vibrational states. Some of the key techniques involve:

1. Energy Attunement: The first step is aligning your energy with that of the cosmic flow. This usually involves a combination of breathwork, meditation, and visualization techniques to attune oneself to higher frequencies.

2. Chakra Balancing: The Pleiadians recognize the chakra system, which is also prevalent in many Earth-based spiritual traditions. They use crystals and visualization techniques to cleanse, balance, and activate these energy centers.

3. Light Infusion: Using visualization, one can draw in light energy from higher dimensions, often visualized as specific colors or frequencies. This 'light infusion' is then directed toward specific intentions, whether for healing, manifestation, or other spiritual objectives.

4. Frequency Tuning: This involves the use of sound,

often through vocal tones, singing bowls, or specific musical scales, to create a vibrational environment conducive to energy work.

Through a harmonious blend of these techniques, Pleiadian energy work aims to fine-tune the energetic body, aligning it more closely with one's higher self and the broader cosmic narrative. The tools and techniques are intended to be modular and adaptable, allowing each Starseed to develop their unique approach to energy work based on their needs and intuitive guidance.

The Synergy Between Crystals and Energy Work

Crystals serve as physical anchors for energy work, aiding in both the focus and amplification of energies. When crystals are employed in energy work, their resonant frequencies interact dynamically with the practitioner's energy field, thus potentiating specific vibrational states conducive to the work at hand. This creates a synergistic feedback loop, where the practitioner's intentions are amplified by the crystal, which in turn elevates the energy field further, leading to more potent outcomes. For instance, using a rose quartz crystal during a love-centered meditation can help amplify feelings of self-love and compassion, making the practice more impactful.

Conclusion

Crystals and energy work stand as two pillars in the spiritual framework of Pleiadian practices. They not only facilitate individual growth and cosmic alignment but also serve as tangible representations of the Pleiadian commitment to harmonizing the material and spiritual realms. As tools for energetic manipulation and spiritual ascension, they exemplify the multifaceted approach Pleiadians have toward achieving higher states of consciousness. They offer a profound yet practical avenue for Pleiadian Starseeds to engage with their spirituality in a grounded, yet ethereal manner, bridging the earthly experience with the cosmic journey that defines their existence.

CHAPTER 4: THE PLEIADIAN PERSPECTIVE ON DEATH AND THE AFTERLIFE

Introduction

As we journey deeper into the spiritual ethos of Pleiadian wisdom, a topic that invariably confronts every sentient being is the subject of death and what comes after. For Pleiadians, and those who identify as Pleiadian Starseeds, understanding death is not merely a philosophical or religious venture but rather an essential component of spiritual growth. Let's delve into the rich tapestry of Pleiadian beliefs and practices surrounding death and the afterlife to better equip ourselves for this inevitable experience.

Pleiadian Beliefs on the Transience of Physical Life

Pleiadians hold a multidimensional view of existence, one in which the physical plane is merely a facet of the broader, intricate spiritual web. They regard physical life as a transient state—a unique but limited opportunity for souls to learn, grow, and contribute to the collective consciousness. In the Pleiadian cosmology, death is not an end but a transformative process that propels the soul into a different state of being.

The moment of death, often described as the "Transition of Light," is considered to be a significant event accompanied by profound spiritual and energetic shifts. During this time, the soul is liberated from its corporeal constraints and commences a journey through various dimensions. Pleiadians emphasize the need to approach this transition with openness and acceptance to enable a smoother passage.

Afterlife Realms and Soul Evolution

After the Transition of Light, it is believed that the soul journeys through an intricate landscape of otherworldly dimensions. These dimensions are not stagnant or fixed but are mutable and highly responsive to the soul's vibrational frequency. Each dimension serves as a realm of learning and soul refinement. The soul has the autonomy to navigate these dimensions based on its level of spiritual maturity, karmic lessons, and readiness for ascension.

At each stage, there are guides, mentors, and beings of higher wisdom who assist the soul. These guides are often soul family members or highly-evolved entities committed to aiding the soul's evolution. Their role is to help the soul assess its experiences, shed any residual negativity or karma, and prepare for either reincarnation or ascension to higher dimensions.

The Pleiadian perspective posits that the soul can choose to reincarnate, not just on Earth but on other planets or dimensions where specific learning experiences await. This rich variety of incarnational choices underpins the Pleiadian understanding of soul evolution as an infinitely expansive, ongoing process.

Preparing for the Transition: Pleiadian Practices

To prepare for the inevitable transition that death brings, Pleiadians engage in specific practices designed to help both the individual and their loved ones. These often include energy work, rituals, and meditative journeys aimed at elevating the soul's frequency. By maintaining a high vibrational state, one is better positioned to navigate the realms of the afterlife and attract experiences that align with their soul's purpose.

Pleiadians also place a strong emphasis on community and collective consciousness in the context of death. It is not uncommon for Pleiadian communities to hold collective meditations or ceremonies when a member is about to transition or has passed away. This is not only to honor the departing soul but also to assist in its spiritual journey through the power of collective intention and love.

The notion of grief, while acknowledged, is reframed as a transitional emotion. Grieving is seen as an opportunity for spiritual growth, for it opens the heart and makes one acutely aware of the impermanence of physical life. The ultimate aim is to transcend grief by understanding death as a new beginning rather than an end.

Summary

The Pleiadian understanding of death and the afterlife is rooted in a multidimensional cosmology that views physical existence as but one chapter in an endless spiritual saga. Death is not an end but a transition, a complex, multi-staged journey that offers the soul opportunities for growth, learning, and ascension. By embracing this holistic view, and by preparing ourselves through specific spiritual practices, we can face the inevitable transition of death with wisdom, grace, and a sense of cosmic continuity. This knowledge not only helps us in our own journey but allows us to support others through the enigmatic portals of death and rebirth.

CHAPTER 5: THE MULTIDIMENSIONAL SOUL: PLEIADIAN BELIEFS ON REINCARNATION

Introduction

In this chapter, we delve into the enigmatic subject of reincarnation as understood from the Pleiadian perspective. As a Pleiadian Starseed, the concept of a multidimensional soul might resonate deeply with you, or perhaps you are just beginning to explore this facet of your spirituality. Regardless, understanding Pleiadian beliefs on reincarnation can provide you with valuable insights into your cosmic purpose, the nature of your soul, and the interconnected web of existence in which we all participate.

The Multidimensional Soul Concept

The Pleiadians propose a revolutionary way to think about the soul that transcends traditional linear understandings of life and death. For them, the soul is not just an ethereal entity confined to a single lifetime. Instead, they view the soul as a multidimensional construct that exists simultaneously across multiple realities, dimensions, and timelines. Imagine your soul as a multifaceted gemstone, with each facet representing a different incarnation, not just on Earth but across galaxies and dimensions.

This multidimensionality implies that our earthly life is just one chapter in a grand, cosmic saga. Your choices, lessons, and experiences here are but a speck in the vast ocean of your soul's journey. It is in this grander context that the Pleiadians emphasize the interconnectedness of all things. In a way, the multidimensional soul embodies the Pleiadian core value of unity and the recognition that we are all connected, not just in this lifetime but through the intricate web of multiple existences.

Reincarnation Cycles and Soul Evolution

According to Pleiadian belief, reincarnation is an evolutionary process designed for soul growth and expansion. As you cycle through various incarnations, you acquire wisdom, develop abilities, and fulfill specific soul contracts or missions. This process is not necessarily linear; you may simultaneously exist in multiple dimensions or life experiences. In each lifetime, your soul assumes a specific vibration to match the learning environment, be it earthly or extraterrestrial.

In this scheme of things, Earth offers a particularly challenging but rewarding environment for soul growth. Its 3D reality, with a unique set of struggles, victories, and complexities, offers a plethora of opportunities for expansion and ascension. The Pleiadians suggest that by incarnating on Earth, you have chosen a potent crucible for the alchemy of your soul, rapidly advancing your evolutionary journey through the experiences and lessons Earthly life provides.

Another notable concept is the 'Soul Family,' groups of souls who are interconnected through multiple lifetimes and dimensions. These groups often incarnate together to assist in mutual learning and to fulfill collective missions. As a Pleiadian Starseed, you might find deep resonance with individuals who are part of your Soul Family, and your encounters with them often feel predestined or extraordinarily synchronistic.

Intersecting with Earthly Understandings

Pleiadian views on reincarnation share some similarities with earthly spiritual traditions, like Hinduism, Buddhism, and various indigenous belief systems, but with the unique twist of cosmic multiplicity and intergalactic connections. While some earthly traditions focus on the karmic cycle of birth and rebirth on this planet alone, Pleiadian spirituality broadens the scope to include cosmic reincarnation cycles.

Their perspective also addresses the concept of "past lives," though from a multidimensional standpoint, the term "concurrent lives" might be more accurate. The soul's multifaceted journeys happen simultaneously in the quantum field, not constrained by earthly perceptions of past, present, and future. Thus, the Pleiadians encourage the exploration of so-called "past life memories" as a means to understand parallel or concurrent experiences your soul is undergoing, contributing to your overall soul evolution.

Conclusion

The Pleiadian perspective on reincarnation offers a multi-layered, interconnected, and cosmic viewpoint on the journey of the soul. Understanding these concepts can vastly expand your awareness of who you are and what you are capable of, enriching your personal and spiritual development. By accepting the idea of a multidimensional soul and reincarnation cycles, not only are you gaining wisdom but you're also aligning closer with the Pleiadian philosophy and your role in the Galactic Family. This alignment could be the key to unlocking further layers of your own multidimensional existence and achieving a greater understanding of your cosmic mission.

PART IV: PLEIADIAN ABILITIES AND GIFTS

CHAPTER 1: TELEPATHY: THE BASICS

Introduction

As we delve deeper into the intriguing realm of Pleiadian abilities and gifts, we encounter one of the most enigmatic and fascinating forms of communication: telepathy. It's a subject that has piqued the interest of many, not just Pleiadian Starseeds, but also humans who sense that communication can be more profound and intricate than just vocalized words. For Pleiadians, telepathy isn't a supernatural phenomenon; it's a natural form of exchanging information that transcends the boundaries of language, distance, and time. In this chapter, we will explore the basics of telepathy from a Pleiadian perspective, how it is cultivated and the significance it holds in Pleiadian culture.

The Essence of Pleiadian Telepathy

To understand Pleiadian telepathy, it's vital to look beyond the popularized sci-fi concepts and delve into the core essence of how it functions. In its simplest form, telepathy is the direct transference of thoughts, emotions, and intentions from one individual to another without the use of conventional senses or external devices. For Pleiadians, telepathy serves as an information conduit that operates in a multi-dimensional framework. It is not merely about reading thoughts but is a more complex process that can involve feeling emotional states, understanding intentions, and even sharing memories.

In the Pleiadian star system, telepathy is introduced at a young age, integrated into educational systems and social practices. It's not considered an extraordinary ability but rather a basic skill, much like learning a language for humans on Earth. The cultivation of telepathic skills not only fosters a more nuanced form of communication but also cultivates empathy and deepens interpersonal relationships.

Cultivating Telepathic Skills

For those who identify as Pleiadian Starseeds and feel a calling to awaken their dormant telepathic abilities, several practices can be useful. The first step is attuning oneself to subtle energies. Much like tuning a radio to catch a specific frequency, one's consciousness needs to be calibrated to receive and send telepathic signals. This involves meditation techniques specifically designed to open and activate the third eye or the 'Anja' chakra, a crucial energy center for psychic abilities.

Moreover, practicing mindfulness can heighten one's sensitivity to subtle shifts in energy and thought patterns. This heightened awareness serves as a fertile ground for telepathic communication. Practicing with a willing partner can be incredibly beneficial, as it allows for real-time feedback and adjustments. It is advised to start with simple exercises such as sending a color, a shape, or a word to each other. Over time, as one becomes more proficient, the complexity of the information exchanged can be increased.

Ethical Considerations

While telepathy opens the door to a form of communication that is incredibly rich and multi-faceted, it also raises essential ethical questions. In a society where thoughts and emotions can be directly accessed, the boundaries of personal privacy become more porous. Pleiadian culture addresses this through strict ethical guidelines that define consent and integrity in telepathic interactions. Telepathy without explicit permission is considered a severe breach of personal space and is socially and morally unacceptable.

Starseeds adapting to telepathic abilities must similarly pay attention to these ethical nuances. Learning to ask for permission energetically and respecting the sanctity of other's inner worlds are crucial steps in the responsible use of this gift.

Summary

Telepathy is more than a form of non-verbal communication; it's a complex interplay of thoughts, emotions, and intentions that transcend the limitations of language. For Pleiadians, it's a natural, integral part of their existence, serving both practical and more profound, relational purposes. Cultivating telepathic abilities involves more than just the activation of certain brain or energetic centers; it requires a holistic approach that integrates mindfulness, ethics, and practice. By doing so, one can not only enhance communication but also deepen the sense of connection with others, thereby enriching the communal fabric in a way that words often fail to capture. Whether you are a Pleiadian Starseed or a human intrigued by the possibilities this skill offers, understanding the basics of telepathy can serve as a gateway to a more interconnected and empathic life.

CHAPTER 2: EMPATHY AND EMOTIONAL HEALING: UNLOCKING YOUR POTENTIAL

Empathy and emotional healing are two of the most cherished and innately developed abilities for Pleiadian Starseeds. These skills can manifest in various ways, often interlinking with one's unique soul mission and the collective evolution of consciousness. This chapter aims to explore the facets of empathic and emotional healing gifts from the Pleiadian perspective, offering guidance on how to harness and cultivate these abilities.

Understanding Empathy in the Pleiadian Context

In Pleiadian culture, empathy is considered more than just the ability to understand and share the feelings of another; it's an advanced form of communication and a vehicle for healing. By being attuned to the emotional and energetic wavelengths of others, Pleiadians engage in a form of intuitive dialogue that transcends spoken words. This advanced empathic ability allows them to not just perceive emotions and energies, but also to transform and heal them.

It's essential to note that empathy, in this galactic context, involves a sophisticated understanding of energetic boundaries. Pleiadian empathy isn't about absorbing the feelings or troubles of others aimlessly; rather, it involves a conscious navigation of emotional landscapes, creating healing spaces while maintaining one's own energetic integrity. For a Pleiadian Starseed, mastering this form of empathy can lead to breakthroughs in self-understanding and collective wellbeing.

Emotional Healing: A Divine Art

In Pleiadian societies, emotional healing is considered a divine art and an essential aspect of their spiritual practices. Unlike earthly approaches, which may involve primarily psychological or therapeutic means, Pleiadian emotional healing is deeply entwined with energy work and spiritual understanding. They believe that emotional wounds are not just mental constructs but are blockages or imbalances in one's energetic body. Clearing these blockages requires a multi-dimensional approach that combines intuitive perception, energetic manipulation, and conscious intention.

For Pleiadian Starseeds on Earth, learning the art of emotional healing involves a balanced integration of earthly and galactic wisdom. Many may find themselves naturally drawn to professions or practices that involve emotional care, such as counseling, psychotherapy, or energy healing modalities like Reiki. Yet, their Pleiadian heritage can imbue these practices with a deeper layer of understanding and efficacy. This doesn't imply that one must become a professional healer; emotional healing is a universal gift that can be applied in every interaction and relationship, fulfilling a vital aspect of the Starseed's galactic mission.

Practical Ways to Unlock Your Empathic and Healing Abilities

While empathy and emotional healing might be innate to many Pleiadian Starseeds, they are skills that can be honed and developed. Here are some practical ways to do so:

1. **Meditative Practices**: Regularly engage in meditative practices that focus on heart-centered consciousness. This can help in fine-tuning your empathic senses.

2. **Emotional Boundaries**: Learn the art of setting emotional and energetic boundaries. This will help you navigate empathy without feeling overwhelmed or drained.

3. **Energy Work**: Familiarize yourself with basic energy work techniques. Understanding chakras, meridians, and energetic fields can provide a foundation for more advanced Pleiadian emotional healing modalities.

4. **Seek Guidance**: If possible, seek mentorship or guidance from those who are experienced in empathic and emotional healing practices, whether they are from earthly traditions or resonate with Pleiadian wisdom.

5. **Mindfulness and Presence**: Cultivate the habit of being fully present in your interactions. This enhances your empathic accuracy and healing abilities.

Empathy and emotional healing are not just gifts but responsibilities for Pleiadian Starseeds. By unlocking and cultivating these abilities, you are fulfilling a vital part of your role within the Galactic Family, contributing to the elevation of consciousness and the healing of collective emotional wounds. Mastering these skills is an ongoing journey, but it's one that can offer profound rewards, not just for yourself, but for the interconnected web of life that spans across dimensions.

CHAPTER 3: ADVANCED INTUITION: TRUSTING YOUR GUT

Intuition is often described as the innate ability to know or understand something without the need for conscious reasoning. It's that subtle whisper, a gut feeling, or a sudden flash of insight that guides you when logic seems to fail. For Pleiadian Starseeds, the aspect of advanced intuition is more than just an occasional guidance system; it's a potent tool deeply embedded in their galactic DNA. This chapter will explore how to recognize, nurture, and master your advanced intuitive abilities, thereby aligning yourself with your Pleiadian origins and tapping into a cosmic reservoir of wisdom.

Recognizing the Signs of Advanced Intuition

As a Pleiadian Starseed, your intuitive capabilities may manifest in a variety of ways that surpass standard human experiences. Often, you might find that your hunches or gut feelings are extraordinarily accurate, defying the probability of mere guesswork. You could also experience frequent synchronicities, such as coming across a certain number sequence, colors, or even meeting individuals who appear just when you're contemplating a particular question. In dreams, you may receive significant messages or insights, not just random subconscious fodder.

Yet another interesting facet is the concept of 'Cosmic Clairvoyance', where you perceive information related to other star systems, galaxies, or dimensions. It's a sort of intuitive telescopic vision that can help you tap into wisdom from far-off realms, often guiding you in your earthly journey. Recognizing these signs is crucial, as it sets the stage for the next steps towards honing this powerful ability.

Nurturing Your Intuitive Sensibilities

1. **Meditation**: Deep, mindful breathing can quieten the chattering mind, allowing your intuition to surface. Pleiadian-guided meditation techniques often involve visualizing the Pleiades star cluster or using gemstones like Larimar and Celestite that are believed to connect with Pleiadian energies.

2. **Journaling**: Writing down your intuitive experiences can help you identify patterns and improve the reliability of your insights. Over time, you can refer back to these entries and notice how your intuitive cues have guided you.

3. **Affirmations**: Positive affirmations can help you build confidence in your intuitive capabilities. For example, saying "I trust my intuition" or "My intuitive skills are a bridge to higher wisdom" can cement the belief in your own abilities.

4. **Practice**: Like any skill, intuition requires regular exercise to develop. Start by making minor decisions based solely on your gut feelings and evaluate the outcomes. Gradually, you can move on to more complex decision-making scenarios.

Advanced Techniques for Mastery

For those who feel comfortable and aligned with their basic intuitive faculties, advanced techniques can be explored. Pleiadian Starseeds often work on fine-tuning their intuitive dialogue by integrating it into their daily lives. For instance, chakra-aligning practices can clear energy blockages and enhance intuitive flow. Pleiadian-specific practices, such as light code activation, can also amplify your intuitive communication channels.

Advanced intuitive abilities can also lead to a deeper exploration of precognition—seeing future events before they happen. While this is a complex skill that requires responsible handling, it can be extremely beneficial in navigating both earthly and galactic challenges. Some Starseeds even integrate their advanced intuition with other abilities like empathy or telepathy for a more holistic experience of their gifts.

Summary

Advanced intuition is a cornerstone in the Pleiadian Starseed's array of abilities. Learning to recognize the signs of this potent skill, nurturing it through various techniques, and advancing its potential to integrate with other gifts can offer you an unprecedented level of wisdom and guidance. Whether you use it to navigate day-to-day decisions or to tap into higher galactic knowledge, your intuition is a celestial compass that continually aligns you with your higher self and the larger Galactic Family. Trusting this internal guidance system can open doors that you never knew existed, and steer you towards fulfilling your earthly mission as part of the Pleiadian lineage.

CHAPTER 4: ENERGY MANIPULATION AND HEALING

Introduction

In our exploration of Pleiadian abilities and gifts, we have covered telepathy, empathy, and advanced intuition. This chapter dives into yet another profound ability that many Pleiadian Starseeds possess—energy manipulation and healing. Understanding this capability is paramount to harnessing your full potential as a Pleiadian being, opening avenues for personal and communal growth, healing, and transformation.

The Nature of Energy Manipulation

Energy manipulation encompasses a range of techniques and practices aimed at harnessing, directing, and transforming energies in the immediate environment and within living organisms. While the term "manipulation" may carry a negative connotation, it is essential to clarify that the Pleiadian understanding of this word emphasizes responsibility and ethical considerations. It is about the benevolent usage of abilities for healing, growth, and advancement, rather than exploitation or harm.

Techniques

Several techniques are central to the practice of energy manipulation, all rooted in Pleiadian traditions. Some of these methods might feel familiar, as Earthly energy practices like Reiki, Qi Gong, and Prana healing share similar elements. Common techniques include:

- **Channeling**: Drawing in cosmic or Earth energy, cleansing it, and channeling it to specific intentions or targets.
- **Balancing**: Realigning the energies within living organisms to achieve homeostasis and optimal functionality. This practice is particularly helpful for emotional or physical healing.
- **Shielding**: Forming protective energy barriers around oneself or others to guard against negative energies or influences.

Tools

Certain Pleiadian tools can assist in energy manipulation:

- **Energy Wands**: These are specialized instruments designed for energy work. They amplify the user's innate abilities and can help direct energies more precisely.
- **Crystals**: Pleiadians have a rich tradition of using crystals for energy manipulation. Each crystal type has specific properties, frequencies, and functions in the practice.

Applications in Healing

One of the most revered applications of energy manipulation is in the field of healing. Pleiadians use their energy manipulation abilities for various therapeutic purposes, both physical and metaphysical.

- **Physical Healing**: Energy manipulation can directly affect the physical body, accelerating cellular repair, improving metabolic functions, and boosting immunity.
- **Emotional Healing**: Energy work is often employed to resolve emotional blockages, traumas, and imbalances, leading to mental well-being.
- **Karmic Healing**: Pleiadian techniques extend to healing karmic cycles, issues from past lives, and ancestral traumas. This work is considered high-level and usually involves advanced practitioners.

Ethical Considerations

Whenever one embarks on using energy for healing, ethical responsibility is paramount. Consent is an essential element, whether explicit or intuitive. It is inappropriate to engage in any form of energy work on someone who has not consented, as this infringes on their free will. Additionally, practitioners need to maintain a balance, ensuring they do not deplete their own energies while performing healing.

Developing Your Abilities

Developing your capacity for energy manipulation and healing involves a combination of study, practice, and mentorship. Pleiadians generally recommend starting with easier techniques, like channeling and balancing, before moving on to more complex tasks such as shielding or karmic healing.

1. **Meditation**: Regular meditation practices help attune your energies and increase sensitivity to the flow of cosmic and Earthly energies.
2. **Mentorship**: If possible, seek out a mentor who can guide you in your energy manipulation journey. A knowledgeable guide can offer invaluable insights and can correct your techniques when necessary.
3. **Ethical Training**: This is crucial for every aspiring energy healer. Understanding the moral and ethical guidelines ensures that your practices are not only effective but also respectful of others' autonomy.

Summary

Energy manipulation and healing form an integral part of the Pleiadian abilities set, offering pathways for personal and collective growth and transformation. These abilities, ranging from channeling and balancing energies to advanced healing techniques, are often innate in Pleiadian Starseeds but can be honed and optimized through disciplined practice and ethical consideration. Whether you aim to heal physical ailments, resolve emotional traumas, or bring about karmic resolutions, this Pleiadian practice holds immense potential for those willing to delve deep into their galactic heritage.

CHAPTER 5: MASTERING ASTRAL PROJECTION

Introduction

The concept of astral projection has long been a topic of fascination in spiritual and metaphysical circles. As a Pleiadian Starseed, you might find that your innate abilities lend themselves naturally to this otherworldly skill. This chapter is aimed at shedding light on the intricacies of astral projection, exploring its relevance from a Pleiadian perspective, and offering some guidance on how you can master this extraordinary talent.

The Fundamentals of Astral Projection

Astral projection is the practice of consciously separating the astral body, or your spiritual form, from the physical body. Unlike dreams or visions, this is a controlled experience that can allow you to explore other realms, communicate with spiritual entities, or even visit the Pleiades in a non-physical form. The practice is not merely an exercise of the imagination; it's a journey that can offer profound insights, healing, and a connection to the greater cosmos.

From a Pleiadian viewpoint, astral projection is not a mystical or elusive practice but rather a natural part of one's multi-dimensional existence. In the Pleiadian star system, this is considered a regular method of travel and interaction, especially when dealing with realms that are less dense than the physical. As a Starseed, you might find that you have an easier time tapping into this ability, even if you are not fully conscious of it.

Techniques for Successful Astral Projection

The act of astral projection can vary greatly in complexity, from beginner-level techniques to advanced methods requiring deep focus and meditation. Here are some foundational steps often recommended for those new to the practice:

1. **Prepare Your Space:** Make sure you're in a quiet, comfortable place where you won't be disturbed. Physical comfort is vital for keeping your mind free from distractions.

2. **Relax Your Body and Mind:** Utilize breathing techniques or progressive muscle relaxation to get into a deeply relaxed state.

3. **Reach a Hypnagogic State:** This is the state between wakefulness and sleep. You might start to notice visual or auditory hallucinations; these are normal and can be a sign that you're on the right track.

4. **Use Visualization:** Once in the hypnagogic state, start visualizing your astral body lifting out of your physical body. Some people use the "rope technique," where they imagine a rope above them that they can use to pull themselves out.

5. **Sever the Astral Cord:** Imagine a silver cord connecting your astral and physical bodies. Mentally sever or unhook this cord to complete the separation. Don't worry; this is symbolic and won't have any

harmful effects.

6. **Explore:** Once you've achieved separation, you're free to explore. Keep in mind that your thoughts and intentions will often guide your experiences, so stay focused on what you wish to accomplish.

Remember, practice makes perfect. You might not be successful on your first try, and that's completely fine. Pleiadian teachings emphasize the value of patience and continual growth.

Pleiadian Perspectives on Astral Projection

In Pleiadian culture, astral projection is often used for various purposes including learning, spiritual growth, and even social interaction. It's not just a tool for individual exploration but also a means for collective consciousness expansion. The collective astral realm, often described as an 'astral meeting place,' is a location where Pleiadians often share knowledge, hold discussions, and even celebrate cosmic events.

Astral projection offers a unique opportunity to reconnect with your Pleiadian heritage. Many Starseeds find that their first successful astral journey is often back to the Pleiadian star system. It's like an internal homing beacon is activated, drawing you back to familiar territories. During such journeys, it's possible to interact with Pleiadian guides or even family members, enhancing your connection and understanding of your galactic lineage.

Conclusion

Astral projection is a profound and enlightening experience that can offer numerous benefits, from self-discovery to cosmic exploration. For Pleiadian Starseeds, mastering this ability can be a part of your spiritual toolkit, providing valuable insights and deepening your connection to the Pleiadian collective. As you practice, you'll likely find that your aptitude for astral projection grows, along with your understanding of your role in the greater cosmic plan. Whether you're a novice or an experienced practitioner, the astral realm offers endless possibilities for growth, learning, and reconnection with your galactic family.

PART V: YOUR CONNECTION TO PLEIADES

CHAPTER 1: IDENTIFYING PLEIADIAN ANCESTRY: SIGNS AND SYNCHRONICITIES

Introduction

As you venture deeper into understanding your role in the galactic family, one of the most captivating journeys is discovering your Pleiadian ancestry. In this context, ancestry doesn't solely mean genetic lineage, but a more complex interplay of soul history, astral connections, and vibrational synchronicities. This chapter aims to guide you in identifying signs and patterns that may indicate your Pleiadian ancestry and the symbolic synchronicities that can affirm your celestial connection.

Signs That You Are a Pleiadian Starseed

Identifying your celestial lineage can be a transformative experience, bringing insights into your purpose, abilities, and the unique characteristics that make you stand out. Here are some signs that suggest a Pleiadian connection:

1. **Innate Wisdom**: From an early age, you have been drawn to spiritual and philosophical subjects that others your age typically do not contemplate. There's a sense that you "know" things that you haven't formally learned.

2. **Intrinsic Empathy**: You have a natural tendency to feel others' emotions deeply, often leading to a life focused on healing and counseling vocations.

3. **Aversion to Conflict**: Pleiadians are known for their peaceful disposition. A clear aversion to violence and conflict can often be a sign of Pleiadian ancestry.

4. **Intuitive and Psychic Abilities**: An almost uncanny ability to sense future events or hidden realities often accompanies Pleiadian lineage. These intuitive faculties can manifest through dreams, visions, or even gut feelings.

5. **Cosmic Fascination**: An innate fascination with the stars, planets, and space exploration often accompanies those with Pleiadian ancestry.

The Role of Synchronicities

Synchronicities serve as confirmatory signals from the universe, often occurring when you are on the verge of a spiritual breakthrough or when you are inquiring about your celestial heritage. These synchronicities can manifest in many ways:

1. **Numerological Patterns**: Sequences like 11:11, 444, or 777 frequently appearing in your life, especially when thinking about your ancestry or spiritual path, can be indicators.

2. **Animal Totems**: Animals appearing in an unusual frequency or in extraordinary circumstances, like a

hawk circling overhead just when you're pondering your celestial roots, can be a form of synchronicity.

3. **Circumstantial Alignments**: Meeting people who share your questions and quests, finding books or courses that exactly match your current inquiries, or hearing the same piece of wisdom from different sources are examples of synchronicities that should not be ignored.

How to Validate Your Connection

While signs and synchronicities are compelling, it's crucial to validate these connections. Meditative journeys into past lives, consulting the Akashic Records, or engaging in astral travel can be effective ways to confirm your Pleiadian ancestry. Moreover, experienced psychics specializing in starseed readings can offer insights into your celestial lineage. Some starseeds have even reported successful validation through regressive hypnotherapy, recalling past experiences or lifetimes in the Pleiades.

Validation is more than an ego-driven curiosity. It's a pathway to understanding your role, your gifts, and your responsibilities as a Pleiadian starseed. Knowing your celestial heritage can profoundly influence your earthly journey, aligning you more closely with your life's purpose and your contributions to the collective consciousness.

Summary

Identifying your Pleiadian ancestry is an enriching experience that offers greater clarity on your unique abilities, inherent wisdom, and cosmic responsibilities. Signs like intrinsic empathy, intuitive faculties, and an aversion to conflict can indicate a Pleiadian lineage. Synchronicities, be it numbers, animals, or circumstantial alignments, often manifest to confirm your celestial connection. While these signs and synchronicities are important indicators, validating your connection through meditation, Akashic readings, or specialized consultations can offer a more comprehensive understanding. As you walk this path, remember that discovering your Pleiadian ancestry is not merely an intellectual exercise, but a transformative journey that aligns you with your higher purpose in both earthly and cosmic realms.

CHAPTER 2: PAST LIVES AND KARMIC CONNECTIONS

Introduction

In your journey as a Pleiadian Starseed, the echoes of your past lives and karmic connections serve as silent guides that subtly influence your current incarnation. Understanding these elements not only offers validation for the experiences and emotions you face but also provides invaluable insights into your higher purpose. In this chapter, we'll delve into the concept of past lives, karmic imprints, and how they interplay in your role within the Galactic Family.

The Multilayered Soul Tapestry

The idea of a soul's reincarnation is central to Pleiadian spirituality. It's envisioned as a tapestry of experiences, woven thread by thread, life by life. Each thread, representing a different incarnation, contributes to the overall design, which is your soul's journey through the cosmos. Your experiences, lessons learned, relationships, and even unresolved issues from these past lives continue to reverberate in your current existence.

These reverberations aren't mere residues; they're active

forces shaping your preferences, relationships, and even your challenges. For example, an inexplicable pull towards certain star systems, planets, or even historical periods on Earth might be your soul's recognition of its previous incarnations. The Pleiadians believe that this kind of 'soul reminiscence' isn't a whimsical daydream but a subconscious memory imprinted onto the essence of your being.

The Karmic Ledger

The word 'karma' may have its roots in Earthly philosophies, but its implications are universal, recognized across dimensions and civilizations. Within the Pleiadian understanding, karma doesn't serve as a system of punishment or reward, but as a cosmic balancing act. Your actions, positive or negative, create energetic imprints that may need to be reconciled in future incarnations.

This reconciliation could manifest in multiple ways. Some Pleiadian Starseeds find themselves born into challenging circumstances to balance the scales of a past life. Others may encounter people who've been part of their soul group for multiple incarnations, sharing intricate karmic relationships that offer both parties opportunities for growth and equilibrium.

For those navigating the intricacies of such karmic connections, awareness is the first step. Once you become aware, you can actively engage in balancing your karmic ledger. Pleiadian spiritual practices often incorporate meditation techniques, energy work, and sacred geometry to facilitate this karmic realignment. The goal isn't to erase or bypass karma but to harmonize with these cosmic forces for a more integrated existence.

Synchronicities as Cosmic Signposts

The universe communicates through symbols and synchronicities, which you might find increasingly noticeable as you awaken to your Pleiadian heritage. These synchronicities often serve as signposts pointing toward unresolved karmic issues or past life connections. It could be a recurring number, a deja vu moment, or even a dream that feels like a distant memory.

Don't dismiss these as random occurrences. Instead, consider them invitations to delve deeper into your spiritual archives. They're cues that there's a pattern, a lesson, or a relationship that requires your attention. By acknowledging these synchronicities, you're not just acting as a passive observer but participating in the co-creative process of your life, shaping your destiny while fulfilling your role in the larger galactic tapestry.

Summary

The relationship between your past lives and current existence is like a river that flows through the landscape of your soul, shaping it in subtle yet profound ways. These past experiences, coupled with the karmic imprints they leave behind, offer a nuanced understanding of your life's purpose, challenges, and connections. By acknowledging these elements, you're better equipped to navigate your role within the Galactic Family. The cosmic dance of karma and reincarnation isn't a loop of endless repetition but a spiral, ever ascending towards higher levels of awareness and integration.

CHAPTER 3: DREAMS AND VISIONS: MESSAGES FROM HOME

Introduction

The world of dreams and visions is a complex tapestry that interweaves elements of the subconscious mind, energetic influences, and multidimensional experiences. For those identifying as Pleiadian Starseeds, dreams and visions can serve as direct conduits for messages from your galactic family, offering guidance, reassurance, and information about your purpose and mission. This chapter will delve into the profound significance of dreams and visions within the Pleiadian context, offering you insight into how to better interpret and engage with these often cryptic but meaningful experiences.

The Nature of Pleiadian Dreams

Dreams, as understood in the Pleiadian perspective, are not mere random sequences created by your mind during sleep. They are complex scenarios, sometimes symbolic and other times literal, that provide avenues for your Higher Self and galactic family to communicate with you. Pleiadian dreams often have recurring themes, specific symbolism, or an unusually vivid clarity that sets them apart from typical dreams.

For example, you might find yourself walking through a surreal landscape that somehow feels more "real" than waking life. Alternatively, you might encounter beings that exude immense love and wisdom, sharing messages through telepathic communication or symbolic gestures. These experiences may serve as validations, triggers for spiritual awakening, or even as instructional platforms where you can learn or train in various skills and understandings.

Interpreting Symbols and Scenarios

Dreams often speak the language of symbols and archetypes. Pleiadian Starseeds may encounter recurring motifs like the Seven Sisters star cluster, known as the Pleiades, exotic landscapes that resemble their home planet, or symbols like certain geometries or color patterns that resonate with Pleiadian frequencies.

Here's a broad approach for interpreting symbols and scenarios:

- **Personal Associations**: Start by examining what the symbols mean to you personally. For instance, if you dream of an ocean, think about your personal emotional connection to the sea. Is it a place of serenity or turbulence for you?
- **Universal Archetypes**: Some symbols have universal meanings rooted in the collective unconscious. For example, water generally represents emotion, and flying might symbolize a desire for freedom.
- **Direct Transmission**: Sometimes, what you see in your dreams could be a more direct form of communication from the Pleiades. These dreams are generally

characterized by a heightened sense of reality and often come with clear, precise messages.

By examining these elements in tandem, you can derive multi-layered interpretations that offer insights into your physical life, spiritual path, or both.

Visions and Altered States of Consciousness

Visions differ from dreams in that they can occur in various states of consciousness, not just during sleep. You may experience visions during meditation, while in nature, or even during moments of great emotional intensity. Unlike dreams, which can be cryptic, visions are often more direct and can provide specific guidance or information.

For Pleiadian Starseeds, these visions can be portals for multidimensional experiences, offering glimpses of parallel realities, future timelines, or past lives. Sometimes, you might even find yourself aboard Pleiadian crafts, participating in galactic meetings, or visiting Pleiadian realms.

Summary

Dreams and visions occupy a place of central importance in Pleiadian spirituality and self-understanding. They serve as interactive interfaces between you and higher dimensions, offering profound insights, messages, and experiences that can assist you in your earthly journey and spiritual evolution. By honing your interpretive skills and nurturing your openness to these experiences, you allow yourself a richer, more informed interaction with your Pleiadian heritage. Remember, your dreams and visions are not mere figments of your imagination; they are messages from home, from a family that watches over you, ever eager to guide and support you on your soul's odyssey.

CHAPTER 4: THE AKASHIC RECORDS: YOUR GALACTIC HISTORY

Introduction

Welcome to another enlightening chapter on your connection to the Pleiades. Here, we delve into a topic that has intrigued spiritual seekers for centuries—the Akashic Records. For Pleiadian Starseeds, the Akashic Records are not just an esoteric concept but a gateway to rediscovering their galactic lineage and history. This chapter will demystify the Akashic Records, exploring how they connect to Pleiadian heritage and how one can access them for personal growth and enhanced cosmic connection.

The Nature of the Akashic Records

Often conceptualized as a cosmic library, the Akashic Records are a repository of every thought, word, action, and experience that has ever occurred, is occurring, or will occur in the Universe. They transcend time and space, existing in an ethereal realm that can be accessed through specialized spiritual techniques. For Pleiadian Starseeds, the Akashic Records serve as an invaluable resource to learn about their soul's past lives, including those in other star systems like the Pleiades.

The Pleiadian connection to the Akashic Records is unique in the sense that Pleiadians often contribute to the Records as keepers or guardians. Some Starseeds may have had incarnations where their primary role was to oversee the storage of cosmic wisdom and experience. Therefore, accessing the Akashic Records can feel not just like a search for knowledge but also like a homecoming.

Accessing the Akashic Records

Accessing the Akashic Records requires a state of deep meditation and focused intention. It is a highly spiritual endeavor and should be approached with utmost respect and readiness. The Records are generally accessed through a 'guide,' often an advanced version of one's higher self or a specialized Akashic Records Keeper. Here are some steps commonly employed to access the Akashic Records:

1. **Preparation**: This involves grounding exercises to align your energies and intentions. You may wish to perform a cleansing ritual or use specific crystals that are attuned to Akashic frequencies, such as amethyst or lapis lazuli.

2. **Deep Meditation**: Here, you enter a meditative state employing techniques that are comfortable to you. Deep, rhythmic breathing usually helps in reaching the right vibrational frequency.

3. **Setting Intention**: Once in a meditative state, you should clearly articulate your intention to access the Akashic Records. It can be an inward articulation or spoken softly.

4. **Meeting the Guide**: In the ethereal realm, you will

meet a guide who will help you navigate the Akashic Records. Be open to receiving any symbols, images, or feelings at this stage.

5. **Accessing Information**: With the assistance of your guide, you can now query the Records. The answers may come in various forms—intuitive knowledge, symbols, or even 'downloads' of information that you understand over time.

6. **Closure**: Always express gratitude to the Akashic Records and your guide, then slowly pull your consciousness back to your physical body.

Pleiadian-Specific Queries in the Akashic Records

For Pleiadian Starseeds, the Akashic Records can offer illuminating insights into their galactic history and mission on Earth. When accessing the Records, one can ask Pleiadian-specific questions such as:

- What is my connection to the Pleiades?
- Have I incarnated in the Pleiades before?
- What was my role in those incarnations?
- What karmic lessons am I carrying from my Pleiadian lives that affect my current Earth life?
- What is my specific mission as a Pleiadian Starseed?

Asking these questions not only expands your understanding of your cosmic heritage but also offers practical guidance in fulfilling your earthly mission as a Pleiadian Starseed.

Summary

The Akashic Records are an invaluable resource for Pleiadian

Starseeds, providing insights into their galactic lineage, past incarnations, and current life mission. Accessing them is a sacred endeavor, requiring specific spiritual techniques and a readiness to delve deep into cosmic wisdom. By successfully navigating the Akashic Records, one can find not just knowledge but a deeper connection to the Pleiades and a clearer understanding of one's role in the grand tapestry of existence.

CHAPTER 5: DEVELOPING A STRONGER CONNECTION: PRACTICES AND TECHNIQUES

In this chapter, we explore the various practices and techniques you can use to deepen your connection with the Pleiadian energies and consciousness. We understand that as a Starseed, you might have experienced moments of loneliness, confusion, or even despair regarding your role and purpose. The aim is to provide you with actionable methods to feel more attuned to your Pleiadian heritage, enhancing your life journey and fulfilling your galactic mission.

Meditation and Visualization Techniques

Meditation has long been a cornerstone of spiritual development and a means for inner exploration. For Pleiadian Starseeds, this takes on additional layers of significance. Pleiadian-guided meditation often involves intricate visualizations of celestial bodies, sacred geometry, and even potential contact with Pleiadian beings.

You can start with simple techniques like grounding, where you visualize roots extending from your body into the Earth. As you progress, you can imagine astral travel to the Pleiades star cluster, experiencing a sense of homecoming and cosmic unity. Over time, these visualizations can become more vivid, leading to deep emotional releases and greater self-awareness.

Meditation often serves as a conduit for downloads, messages, or activations that are Pleiadian in origin. You may even find yourself channeling information or experiencing revelations about your past lives, galactic history, or mission on Earth.

Frequency Alignment and Energy Work

Your energetic body, or auric field, is like a multi-dimensional tapestry woven with the essence of your Pleiadian lineage. To better connect with this aspect of yourself, consider engaging in frequency alignment exercises. This entails working with various vibrational tools like singing bowls, tuning forks, or even specially attuned music that resonates with Pleiadian frequencies.

Reiki, crystal healing, and light language activations are other potent forms of energy work you can use. These modalities can serve to cleanse any blockages in your system and elevate your vibratory state, aligning you more closely with Pleiadian energies. The idea is not to force a connection but to allow the natural affinity between you and your Pleiadian origins to unfold harmoniously.

Rituals and Sacred Spaces

Creating a sacred space can serve as a physical manifestation of your intent to connect more deeply with your Pleiadian lineage. This space can include symbols, crystals, or artifacts that hold particular meaning for you and evoke a sense of the divine or the cosmic. Pleiadian symbols, star maps, and representations of the Seven Sisters (the brightest stars in the Pleiades cluster) can be particularly powerful.

Within this sacred space, you can perform rituals that resonate with you. This could range from simply lighting a candle while meditating to more elaborate rituals involving invocations, chants, and the use of elemental energies. These rituals act as markers in the energetic realm, signifying your commitment and openness to receive guidance, wisdom, and love from Pleiadian entities.

Summary

Developing a deeper connection to your Pleiadian heritage is a process that takes time, intention, and practice. However, the rewards are multi-faceted and far-reaching, extending from your spiritual and emotional well-being to a richer understanding of your cosmic purpose. Techniques like meditation, frequency alignment, and the use of rituals and sacred spaces are all valuable tools that can pave the way for a more intimate and fulfilling relationship with your Pleiadian self. As you delve into these practices, you not only honor your lineage but also enrich your earthly life with higher wisdom and spiritual clarity. The end goal is not merely to recognize your Pleiadian connection but to live it fully, integrating these expansive dimensions of your being into your daily human experience.

PART VI: MEETING OTHER STARSEEDS

CHAPTER 1: FINDING YOUR SOUL FAMILY

Introduction

You've arrived at a critical juncture in your galactic journey—meeting other starseeds. The soul family you seek is not just an abstract concept but a tangible pillar of support and spiritual enrichment. Whether they hail from the Pleiadian star system or other celestial realms, these kindred spirits resonate at a frequency remarkably close to yours. They provide you with the sense of belonging and understanding that is often hard to find in the hustle and bustle of Earth life. But how do you find them? How do you recognize them? These are the central questions we shall delve into in this chapter.

Recognizing the Signs and Synchronicities

Recognition often comes in fleeting moments—glimpses of profound connection that defy logic or explanation. When you meet a member of your soul family, there is often an immediate sense of comfort, a feeling of having known this person for lifetimes. The conversation flows effortlessly, and an undeniable mutual respect prevails, even in the face of disagreements or differences of opinion. Your energies intermingle in a dance of familiarity and resonance.

Interestingly, you might also experience déjà vu or

synchronicities around these individuals. Perhaps you meet under unusual or inexplicable circumstances, like running into them multiple times in one day or encountering them right after having a vivid dream or premonition. These are more than mere coincidences; they are the universe's way of alerting you to the presence of someone significant in your cosmic journey.

Utilizing Pleiadian Tools for Connection

The Pleiadian tradition offers various tools and practices to facilitate the discovery of your soul family. For instance, one could engage in guided meditations specifically designed to connect you with the energies of your soul family members, even before you meet them physically. These meditative sessions often incorporate visualization techniques and may employ the use of Pleiadian symbols or crystals to magnify the experience.

Similarly, another approach would involve astral projection or remote viewing techniques, where you temporarily step out of your physical body to meet and interact with members of your soul family in the astral realm. Such ethereal meetings can sometimes offer insights or clues about how and where to encounter these individuals in the physical world.

Starseed Gatherings and Online Platforms

In this age of technological advancement, the internet has emerged as a powerful tool for connecting like-minded individuals, including starseeds. There are online forums, social media groups, and even dedicated websites that serve as platforms for starseeds to share experiences, wisdom, and support. Some starseeds also find it helpful to attend events, workshops, or retreats centered around spiritual and metaphysical topics. These gatherings can be pivotal in connecting you with members of your soul family.

In addition to virtual interactions, in-person starseed gatherings can be especially potent. Such assemblies often employ collective meditation, energy healing, and other group activities designed to amplify the spiritual energies of the participants. Being in the physical presence of other starseeds can trigger activations, accelerate spiritual growth, and facilitate a deeper level of connection than might be possible through online platforms alone.

Summary

Finding your soul family is a transformative experience that adds a deeper layer of meaning to your Earthly and galactic existence. It's often a journey of recognizing signs and synchronicities, utilizing Pleiadian tools for enhanced connection, and leveraging both online and offline platforms to meet like-minded individuals. The shared experiences, wisdom, and emotional support that you gain from your soul family are invaluable resources on your path of spiritual evolution and self-discovery. So open your heart and your senses to these profound connections, for they are essential milestones on your cosmic journey.

CHAPTER 2: THE IMPORTANCE OF COMMUNITY

As a Pleiadian Starseed, you might find yourself in a perpetual search for something more, a yearning for a sense of belonging that goes beyond the earthly ties of family and friends. Understanding the significance of community, especially among Starseeds and spiritually like-minded individuals, can make a profound difference in your life journey. In this chapter, we will explore why community matters, how it can support your galactic mission, and how to nurture these special connections.

The Spiritual Symbiosis

Being part of a community provides an ecosystem for mutual growth and spiritual ascension. In a world where the mainstream might not readily accept the ideas and experiences common to Starseeds, having a safe space to share, learn, and grow is essential. Within a Starseed community, the collective wisdom and the support network act as catalysts for personal and galactic endeavors. There is an energetic exchange that takes place, almost like a spiritual symbiosis, where each member amplifies the other's frequencies, opening new doors for growth and awareness.

Not only does being part of a community offer emotional and intellectual support, but it can also facilitate powerful joint energetic ventures, such as group meditations and healings. These activities, often much more potent when performed as a collective, can have ramifications not just for the individuals involved but for the planet and beyond. Starseeds often have missions that involve raising the Earth's vibration, and being in a community amplifies the impact you can have on these higher-level objectives.

Co-Creating Reality

Within a community, you are not just a passive member but an active co-creator of your shared reality. This involves a conscious effort to build each other up, contributing unique skills, insights, and energies to serve the collective goal. Whether you are healers, intuitives, or have unique abilities related to energy manipulation, each Starseed brings something to the table. As you give and receive, you activate latent talents not just in yourself but in others as well.

This is particularly important for Pleiadian Starseeds, who are often guided by a sense of altruism and a desire to see others grow. In co-creating reality, you are fulfilling both a personal and a collective mission, honing your abilities and helping others in their own path of ascension. Given the innate Pleiadian traits of empathy and sensitivity, the benefits of this mutual upliftment are often felt at a profound emotional level, offering validation and resonance that can be hard to find in traditional social settings.

Challenges and Conscious Engagement

While the benefits of being in a community are immense, it's important to be aware of the challenges that can arise.

Energetic imbalances, conflicts of interest, or diverging paths can sometimes create discord. The key to a harmonious Starseed community lies in conscious engagement. This means actively participating in the well-being of the group, resolving conflicts through heart-centered dialogue, and being attuned to the collective energy.

For Pleiadian Starseeds, this also means being aware of your emotional boundaries. Your heightened empathy can sometimes lead to taking on collective energies too deeply, which might be overwhelming. Learning how to manage your energies and protect your vibrational field is crucial when engaging with any community, especially one as energetically charged as a Starseed collective.

Summary

Community is not just a supplementary aspect of the Starseed experience; it is a cornerstone. By participating in a community, you gain access to a wellspring of knowledge, experience emotional and energetic support, and find a platform to live out your greater cosmic role. For Pleiadian Starseeds, who are often drawn to humanitarian and uplifting missions, the community becomes an extension of their very essence, a sacred space where they can truly be themselves while serving a higher purpose. Conscious engagement, mutual respect, and energetic exchange are the keys to maintaining a community that not only sustains its members but acts as a beacon of light for the broader cosmic family.

CHAPTER 3: NAVIGATING RELATIONSHIPS WITH NON-STARSEEDS

Introduction

As Pleiadian Starseeds continue to awaken and find their soul families and communities, they must also navigate the nuanced relationships they have with those who don't identify as Starseeds. The world is filled with individuals with a wide array of backgrounds, beliefs, and energies, and learning to coexist with everyone is crucial. This chapter aims to guide you through the intricacies of these relationships, offering insights on how to maintain balance, understanding, and mutual respect.

Bridging the Gap: Emotional and Intellectual Understanding

One of the first things to remember is that the experiences and wisdom you possess as a Starseed may not be easily understood or accepted by those who don't share your origins or perspectives. This often results in a gap, both emotional and intellectual, between Starseeds and non-Starseeds. The first step in bridging this gap is through communication that employs emotional intelligence.

When engaging in discussions that delve into your experiences, beliefs, or feelings, it's crucial to be aware of the other person's emotional cues. Pay attention to their body language, expressions, and tone of voice to gauge their comfort level. If you sense skepticism, defensiveness, or even fear, it may be wise to either shift the topic or clarify your point in a way that makes it more relatable to earthly experiences.

Intellectually, try not to overwhelm non-Starseeds with too many concepts or terminology that they might not understand. Focus instead on the foundational ideas that can resonate with most people. Concepts of love, community, spiritual growth, and ethical considerations, for example, can be common grounds where you can meet and share ideas.

Navigating Emotional Sensitivities

As a Pleiadian Starseed, you may have heightened empathic abilities, allowing you to feel the emotions of those around you intensely. This can be both an asset and a challenge when interacting with non-Starseeds, who may not understand the depths of your emotional sensitivity. It's common for Starseeds to feel misunderstood or overwhelmed by the harsh energies or emotional baggage carried by others. Therefore, it is crucial to set energetic boundaries to protect your emotional well-being.

One practice that can be helpful is to imagine a bubble of protective light around you when you are in emotionally charged situations. This light can act as a filter, allowing only positive energy to enter your aura. With this protective barrier, you can be emotionally present in your interactions without being drained or influenced by other people's energies.

Additionally, recognize the signs of emotional fatigue and take time for self-care. Activities like meditation, nature walks, or simply spending time alone can recharge your emotional batteries and prepare you for future interactions.

Sharing Wisdom Without Imposing Beliefs

There's a fine line between sharing your wisdom as a Pleiadian Starseed and imposing your beliefs on others. The key to navigating this is consent and receptivity. Always sense if the other person is open to hearing what you have to say. Sometimes the best way to share wisdom is not through words but by example. Your actions, guided by your Pleiadian ethics and values, can speak volumes and attract people who are genuinely interested in understanding your worldview.

It's also important to approach these discussions with humility. Remember that wisdom is not exclusive to Starseeds; it exists in all cultures, philosophies, and individual experiences. Be open to learning from non-Starseeds as much as you are keen on sharing your own wisdom. This exchange can be enriching for both parties and can foster a deeper understanding and respect for each other's unique paths.

Summary

Navigating relationships with non-Starseeds can be a complex but rewarding journey. By employing emotional intelligence, setting energetic boundaries, and sharing wisdom respectfully, you can enrich your interactions and contribute to a collective environment of understanding and growth. These relationships offer an invaluable opportunity to practice compassion, tolerance, and the harmonious integration of diverse perspectives, which are essential skills not just for your earthly life but for fulfilling your broader galactic mission.

CHAPTER 4: BALANCING HUMAN LIFE WITH GALACTIC COMMITMENTS

Introduction

The life of a Pleiadian Starseed often requires a juggling act between the mundane aspects of earthly life and the higher vibrational commitments that come with being part of a Galactic Family. This chapter explores strategies for maintaining that balance, so you can fulfill your earthly responsibilities without neglecting your spiritual and galactic duties.

The Earthly Realm: Jobs, Relationships, and Responsibilities

The 3D reality of Earth comes with a set of tasks and obligations that most humans find unavoidable: employment, relationships, community involvement, and self-care among them. For Starseeds, these tasks can sometimes feel like burdens, distractions from the more transcendent aspects of existence. However, it is crucial to remember that your incarnation on Earth serves specific purposes that include engaging with the earthly plane.

1. **Employment**: Choosing a career that aligns with your Starseed mission can make your earthly experience far more fulfilling. Occupations in healing, arts, sciences, or social work are often well-suited for Starseeds.
2. **Relationships**: Interpersonal relationships serve as vital learning grounds for Starseeds. While they might find more natural kinship among other Starseeds, interactions with non-Starseeds offer valuable lessons in empathy, patience, and unconditional love.
3. **Community and Worldly Obligations**: Engaging in social and environmental causes can align well with the Starseed's instinctual desire to "heal the world."

The Galactic Commitment: Awakening, Ascension, and Activation

Being a Starseed is not just an identity but a responsibility. Your soul contract often includes various tasks and commitments at the galactic level.

1. **Awakening and Ascension**: Your own spiritual awakening is not only for personal growth but serves as a beacon for others. The vibrational increase you attain can help uplift the collective.
2. **Activation**: Starseeds are often involved in work that includes energy activations, either of places, other beings, or even planetary grids. This work can be both physically taxing and time-consuming.
3. **Galactic Family Responsibilities**: You may have tasks that involve direct interaction with your Pleiadian family. This could range from astral meetings to receiving downloads of crucial information that you need to share.

Finding a Balanced Path: Strategies and Considerations

Navigating between your earthly life and galactic commitments can be challenging, but it's possible to find a balanced path through thoughtful planning and self-awareness.

1. **Time Management**: Allocate specific time for your galactic work, just as you would for any earthly job or commitment. Your galactic tasks are a significant part of your life's mission, and they deserve devoted time.
2. **Boundaries**: Learning to say no is essential, both in your earthly and galactic commitments. Overcommitting in either realm will result in burnout and ineffectiveness.
3. **Integration**: The more you can integrate your earthly and galactic lives, the smoother your journey will be. For instance, using your spiritual gifts in your earthly occupation or applying your worldly skills in your galactic tasks can create a seamless experience.

Summary

Balancing your earthly and galactic commitments can sometimes feel like walking a tightrope. Yet, both are integral parts of your life's mission and should not be neglected. Finding employment that aligns with your mission, engaging in meaningful relationships, and contributing to worldly causes can satisfy your earthly responsibilities. Meanwhile, your galactic commitments can be managed through adequate time allocation, maintaining clear boundaries, and integrating your earthly and cosmic lives. By achieving this balance, you not only fulfill your duties but also lead a richer, more harmonious life.

CHAPTER 5: THE PLEIADIAN COMMUNITY ON EARTH

Introduction

While the journey of a Pleiadian Starseed can often feel solitary, given the unique path you are treading, it is essential to remember you are not alone. In fact, a growing number of Pleiadian Starseeds are actively building communities on Earth. This chapter explores the contours of these emerging Pleiadian communities, how they differ from mainstream society, and what role they aim to play in the collective consciousness.

The Growth of Pleiadian Communities

Since the dawn of the 21st century, there has been an upsurge in the number of individuals identifying as Starseeds, specifically from the Pleiadian star system. Many of these individuals have been instinctively drawn to each other, forming tight-knit communities both online and in physical spaces. These communities serve multiple purposes:

1. **Knowledge Sharing**: Pleiadian communities are often

the focal points for pooling resources, experiences, and insights into the Pleiadian way of life, spirituality, and purpose on Earth. In such gatherings, newer Starseeds can quickly catch up on their understanding of their roles and missions.

2. **Emotional Support**: Given that Pleiadian Starseeds often feel like outsiders in mainstream society, these communities provide emotional scaffolding. They serve as safe spaces where individuals can be their authentic selves without judgment.

3. **Collective Efforts**: Many Pleiadian communities also participate in collective spiritual activities. This could range from group meditations to sending healing energies to troubled spots on Earth. These activities not only strengthen the community but also amplify the impact of their spiritual work.

The Pleiadian Lifestyle on Earth

A typical Pleiadian community on Earth may diverge significantly from what is considered "normative" in the surrounding culture. These differences manifest in various ways:

- **Holistic Living**: Pleiadian communities often embrace a lifestyle that is more in sync with nature, preferring holistic health methods, clean eating, and sustainable living.
- **Spiritual Practices**: You will find that spiritual pursuits are deeply interwoven into the daily routines of these communities. These could include but are not limited to, morning meditations, energy healing sessions, and frequent discussions on spiritual topics.
- **Inclusive Values**: A defining feature of these

communities is the accent on inclusivity, compassion, and mutual respect. Hierarchies are minimal, and decision-making is often collaborative, relying on the wisdom of the collective rather than a single leader.

- **Interstellar Communication**: Advanced members of Pleiadian communities often engage in efforts to maintain contact with Pleiadian guides or the Galactic Federation, seeking guidance or offering Earthly updates. This makes these communities dynamic and continuously evolving.

Challenges and Road Ahead

While the growth and development of Pleiadian communities on Earth is heartening, there are challenges:

- **Social Perception**: Due to their unconventional beliefs and lifestyle, Pleiadian communities often face misunderstandings or even ridicule from mainstream society.
- **Internal Conflicts**: Like any community, Pleiadian gatherings are not immune to disagreements or conflicts, often stemming from different interpretations of Pleiadian teachings or missions.
- **Ethical Questions**: As these communities grow in influence, questions about ethical responsibilities also arise, especially concerning the dissemination of Pleiadian wisdom and how it interacts with Earth's existing systems.

Despite these challenges, Pleiadian communities are poised to play a significant role in the Great Awakening and the Ascension Process, serving as oases of higher-frequency energies and wisdom on Earth. They act as pockets of 5D consciousness in a predominantly 3D world, and their influence is expected to grow exponentially in the coming years.

Summary

The Pleiadian communities on Earth represent microcosms of Pleiadian energies and wisdom, serving as sanctuaries for Starseeds and seekers alike. Despite challenges from both within and outside these communities, their growth and influence are a testament to the awakening of human consciousness to galactic realities. As a Pleiadian Starseed, finding or even forming such a community can significantly aid your mission on Earth, offering both the support and the collective energy to propel you on your spiritual journey.

PART VII: STARSEED ACTIVATIONS

CHAPTER 1: ACTIVATION CODES: WHAT THEY ARE AND HOW TO USE THEM

Introduction

In your ongoing journey as a Pleiadian Starseed, you may encounter specific tools designed to awaken dormant aspects of your consciousness, elevate your spiritual understanding, and help align you with your galactic mission. One of these powerful tools is the use of activation codes. This chapter delves deeply into what activation codes are, their historical context within the Pleiadian culture, and the practical applications for using them to enhance your life and spiritual growth.

The Nature of Activation Codes

Activation codes are essentially sequences of numbers, letters, symbols, or sounds that serve as keys to unlock specific energies, frequencies, or understanding. They are a bit like cosmic passwords, granting access to concealed or dormant aspects of your soul's blueprint. These codes are intentionally embedded in our energetic field by our higher selves or are handed down from Pleiadian guides and teachers. They function as tools for the activation of our DNA, the opening of psychic abilities, and the development of our higher faculties, such as intuition, clairvoyance, and telepathy.

While some may view these codes as mere sequences of characters, within the Pleiadian understanding, they are alive with intention and purpose. Each element within the code vibrates at a specific frequency and resonates with particular aspects of the Universe, including celestial bodies, cosmic events, and interdimensional realms. Thus, the code acts as a conduit, a bridge between your current state and the state you aim to achieve.

Historical Context in Pleiadian Culture

In Pleiadian culture, activation codes have been in use for millennia. They are traditionally imparted during sacred ceremonies and initiations, where individuals are prepared to receive these codes at different levels of their spiritual maturation. Some codes are common and shared among community members, designed to enhance collective frequencies and galactic coherence. Others are highly personalized, tailored to an individual's unique vibratory signature and life mission.

These codes are considered sacred and are often passed down through lineages, both biological and spiritual. They serve as milestones within an individual's spiritual journey, marking significant shifts and awakenings. Notably, some of the most revered Pleiadian scholars, healers, and leaders have cited the role of activation codes in their profound shifts of consciousness, allowing them to access ancient wisdom, develop healing abilities, and establish deeper connections with other cosmic civilizations.

Practical Applications

Now, let's turn to how you can employ these activation codes in your life. To begin with, it's essential to approach the use of activation codes with reverence and intentionality. Mindlessly reciting or meditating upon these codes will not yield the desired results. Instead, one must approach them as a partnership between your present self and the potentialities of your higher self, held within the code like a seed waiting to sprout.

1. **Identification of Codes:** To find the codes meant for you, engage in spiritual practices like meditation, dream journaling, and astral travel. These codes may also be received during energy healing sessions or revealed through intuition or clairvoyant experiences.

2. **Integration Process:** Once you have identified your activation codes, the next step is to integrate them into your energetic system. This can be done through repeated recitations, embedding them in your daily prayers, or meditating upon them.

3. **Active Usage:** As you become comfortable with your activation codes, you may begin to utilize them in different areas of your life, like focusing on a code for abundance during a business venture, or a code for emotional healing during challenging times.

4. **Monitoring Results:** It's critical to monitor the effects these codes have on your mental, emotional, and spiritual state. Some people experience immediate shifts, while for others, the transformation is gradual.

Summary

Activation codes are a vital aspect of Pleiadian spiritual technology, serving as cosmic keys to unlock latent potentials within us. Rooted deeply in Pleiadian history, they have been used for ages to facilitate spiritual growth, activate dormant abilities, and align individuals with their life missions. Practical application involves a multi-step process of identification, integration, active usage, and result monitoring. As you work with these codes, it is crucial to remain conscious of your experiences, making adjustments as necessary, and maintaining a deep sense of reverence for this ancient and sacred practice.

CHAPTER 2: THE IMPORTANCE OF SOLAR AND LUNAR EVENTS

Introduction

In the context of Starseed activations, solar and lunar events play a pivotal role that may be underestimated by those not familiar with the energy systems linked to celestial movements. These cosmic occurrences, such as solar flares, lunar eclipses, and even regular phases of the moon, can serve as potent windows of opportunity for Starseeds—especially Pleiadian Starseeds—to align with their highest potential and initiate profound transformations. This chapter aims to delve deeply into the mechanisms by which these celestial events influence Starseed activations and provide practical insights for harnessing this cosmic energy.

Cosmic Resonance and Starseed Activations

The Pleiadian understanding of cosmic resonance posits that all celestial bodies emanate specific frequencies that interact with each other in a dynamic dance. Imagine the universe as a grand symphony, where each instrument contributes to the creation of harmonious (and sometimes dissonant) melodies. In this vast cosmic orchestra, solar and lunar events serve as pivotal moments—think of them as crescendos or key modulations—that bring about shifts in the energy fields of celestial bodies, including Earth.

When a solar flare erupts or a lunar eclipse occurs, the change in frequency is not merely confined to the celestial bodies directly involved. It ripples across the cosmos, affecting the energetic constitution of all beings sensitive to these shifts. For Starseeds, these events act like cosmic keys that can unlock latent abilities, clear karmic debris, or even re-align them with their life mission. Essentially, these cosmic occurrences offer 'gaps' in the conventional space-time fabric, which can be capitalized upon for accelerated growth and spiritual alignment.

Harnessing the Energy of Solar and Lunar Events

Solar Events

Solar flares, eclipses, and other activities on the Sun's surface unleash a tremendous amount of energy, which impacts the Earth's magnetosphere and, consequently, all life forms on the planet. Pleiadian Starseeds, with their heightened sensitivity to energy shifts, can find these periods particularly activating. During significant solar events, practices such as meditation, grounding exercises, and energy work can be exponentially more potent.

A helpful approach during solar activities is to focus on the third eye and heart chakras. The reason for this lies in the affinity of solar energy with the principles of insight and unconditional love. A simple visualization technique involves imagining a golden beam of light descending from the Sun, entering through the crown chakra, and filling the entire body with radiant energy. This serves not just as an activation, but also a purification process.

Lunar Events

The moon, with its cyclic phases, has been a symbol of emotional and subconscious realms in various cultures. Lunar events like full moons, new moons, and lunar eclipses have unique energetic imprints. Full moons often relate to culmination and emotional release, new moons to initiation and beginnings, and eclipses to transformation and abrupt shifts.

To harness lunar energy, Starseeds can focus on the sacral and root chakras, which are centers for emotional balance and earthly connection, respectively. Lunar energies assist in deep emotional healing and can be channeled for enhancing psychic abilities like clairvoyance and empathy. Moonlight baths, where one stands or sits under the moon, absorbing its silvery light, can act as powerful activation rituals during these times.

Conclusion

Understanding the importance of solar and lunar events in the context of Starseed activations opens up a wealth of opportunities for growth and transformation. These cosmic occurrences serve as amplifiers, magnifying the potential for inner work and energetic alignment. By consciously engaging with these energies through targeted practices, Pleiadian Starseeds can accelerate their spiritual evolution, unlock latent gifts, and come closer to fulfilling their roles within the Galactic Family. As above, so below; as the universe shifts, so do we. The key lies in recognizing these moments of cosmic resonance and utilizing them as the unique opportunities for activation that they truly are.

CHAPTER 3: STARSEED SYMBOLS AND SIGILS: UNLOCKING YOUR GIFTS

Introduction

In your quest to fully grasp your role as a Pleiadian Starseed and to activate your latent abilities, understanding the symbology associated with this cosmic lineage can be particularly transformative. Symbols and sigils act as keys to higher realms of consciousness, providing a language that transcends spoken or written forms. In the Pleiadian context, these sacred geometries are not mere drawings; they are potent energetic imprints that can catalyze deep spiritual awakenings and activate hidden capabilities.

The Functionality of Symbols and Sigils

Symbols and sigils can be likened to energy conduits, connecting the physical and non-physical realms. In Pleiadian lore, they are often related to specific frequencies of light and sound, designed to resonate with the intricate structure of your DNA. When activated, these symbols can:

1. Facilitate Healing: The energetic vibration of certain symbols can catalyze internal healing processes, whether it's emotional traumas or physical ailments.

2. Activate Latent Abilities: Some symbols serve as catalysts for awakening dormant psychic and intuitive capabilities, such as clairvoyance or telepathy.

3. Enhance Spiritual Connectivity: Utilizing certain sigils can amplify your spiritual connections, making it easier to communicate with higher dimensions, including contact with Pleiadian beings.

These functionalities are not rigid compartments but interact in complex ways, making each experience highly individualistic. Importantly, while these symbols are potent, they are not a substitute for inner work. Think of them as tools that can amplify and guide your inner spiritual endeavors.

Types of Pleiadian Symbols and Sigils

It is worth noting that Pleiadian symbology is vast, reflecting the rich spiritual traditions and advanced understanding of sacred geometry that this civilization possesses. Here are some types you may come across:

1. **Activation Codes:** These are intricate symbols often presented in a series or grid. When meditated upon, they can awaken specific energetic pathways within you, opening the door to higher capabilities.

2. **Healing Sigils:** These are specially designed for therapeutic aims. When focused upon during meditation or applied to particular chakra points, they can invoke specific frequencies conducive to healing.

3. **Transmutation Symbols:** These are employed for

altering energy dynamics, either within oneself or in the external environment. They are particularly useful in cleansing spaces or auras.

How to Utilize Pleiadian Symbols and Sigils

The application of these symbols is as much an art as it is a science. Here are some general guidelines:

1. **Intuitive Resonance:** Choose symbols or sigils that resonate with you at an intuitive level. Your resonance is an indication of energetic alignment.
2. **Sacred Space:** Before engaging with the symbols, create a sacred space that promotes concentration and energetic purity. This could be an altar or simply a quiet room.
3. **Intention Setting:** Clearly state your intentions before initiating interaction with the symbols. This will help channel the energies more effectively.
4. **Meditative Focus:** Meditate upon the symbol, allowing your consciousness to merge with its geometrical intricacies. Imagine the symbol being illuminated, its light frequencies interacting with your energetic field.
5. **Integration:** After your session, give yourself time to integrate the energies. You may also record any insights, visions, or feelings that arose during your interaction with the symbol.

Summary

Symbols and sigils offer a unique medium for Pleiadian Starseeds to connect with their galactic lineage, unlock hidden gifts, and expedite their spiritual evolution. Whether it is activation codes designed to awaken specific abilities, healing sigils focused on therapeutic outcomes, or transmutation symbols for altering energy dynamics, each has a specific role in your spiritual toolbox. The effectiveness of these symbols is enhanced when they are used in alignment with your intuitive resonance, within a sacred space, and with clear intentions. Remember, these are facilitators of transformation, not shortcuts. Your commitment to inner work remains the cornerstone of your galactic journey.

CHAPTER 4: ACTIVATION MEDITATIONS

Introduction

Meditation is a potent tool for mental clarity, emotional balance, and spiritual awakening. However, when it comes to Starseeds, particularly those of Pleiadian origin, meditation serves an even more profound purpose: activation. Activation meditations can awaken dormant abilities, strengthen your galactic connection, and align you more closely with your cosmic purpose. This chapter delves into various techniques, rituals, and contemplative practices that are designed to stimulate and unlock your Pleiadian potentials.

Types of Activation Meditations

Energetic Channeling Meditation

This meditation type aims at channeling the cosmic energies from the Pleiades star cluster to activate your internal energy systems. It often involves visualizing a flow of luminescent energy descending from the Pleiades into your crown chakra, permeating every cell and awakening your DNA. This not only uplifts your vibrational frequency but also assists in manifesting Pleiadian traits more fully.

Merkaba Activation Meditation

The Merkaba is a geometrical shape, a star tetrahedron, considered to be the divine light vehicle. In Pleiadian spirituality, activating your Merkaba is akin to turning on a cosmic switch, connecting you more deeply to your galactic origins. The meditation revolves around intricate visualization techniques, where you imagine your Merkaba rotating around you, integrating your physical and light bodies.

DNA Activation Meditation

In Pleiadian belief systems, a significant portion of human DNA is dormant, often referred to as "junk DNA" in conventional science. However, it is thought that these "dormant" strands contain the keys to our true Pleiadian essence. DNA Activation Meditation focuses on stimulating these sleeping strands, bringing them online through intention, visualization, and frequency modulation. This is usually accompanied by vocal toning or sound healing methods, such as binaural beats or Solfeggio frequencies.

The Role of Intention and Focus

The element that bridges all forms of activation meditations is intention. Without a clear, directed focus, the meditation turns into a passive exercise rather than an active transformation. Starseeds must approach these meditations with defined goals, be it awakening psychic abilities, enhancing emotional empathy, or attaining spiritual enlightenment. Your intention acts as the compass that guides the activating energies to the right doors within your inner self, unlocking them for your broader cosmic journey.

Another aspect of focus involves maintaining uninterrupted attention during the meditation. The Pleiadian energies you are channeling are of a high vibrational nature, requiring a concentrated effort to integrate. Any distractions or mental wanderings can dilute the effectiveness of the meditation. Some practitioners use physical objects like crystals, aligned with Pleiadian frequencies, as focal points to help sustain attention during the process.

Practical Tips for Effective Activation Meditations

1. **Sacred Space**: Create a peaceful, uncluttered space for your meditation practice. This sets the stage for higher vibrations to circulate.
2. **Timing**: Aligning your meditations with cosmic events like lunar cycles or solar flares can amplify their effectiveness.
3. **Duration**: While there's no set time, it's advisable to meditate for at least 20-30 minutes for substantial energetic shifts to occur.
4. **Guidance**: For beginners, guided meditations, either from trusted mentors or reliable sources, can offer a structured pathway into activation practices.
5. **Post-Meditation Integration**: After concluding your session, spend a few moments grounding yourself, as the energies can be potent. Drinking water, consuming light foods, or simply walking barefoot on the earth can assist in this.

Summary

Activation meditations are an indispensable tool for Pleiadian

Starseeds looking to awaken their dormant capabilities and fortify their connection with their galactic family. These aren't just ordinary meditation techniques; they are tailored to align you with cosmic frequencies that stimulate and activate your inner potential. Through a combination of specific visualization methods, intent focus, and practical considerations, you can use activation meditations as a gateway to your higher Pleiadian self. As you delve into these practices, remember that patience is key. Awakening is a journey, not a destination, and each meditation brings you closer to your ultimate role in the galactic family.

CHAPTER 5: LIGHT LANGUAGE: THE GALACTIC TONGUE

Introduction

In this chapter, we venture into the mysterious yet captivating realm of Light Language—the "Galactic Tongue" understood by Pleiadian Starseeds and other advanced cosmic entities. As we explore this intricate form of communication, we'll delve into its origins, functionalities, and how it serves as a powerful tool for Starseed activations and spiritual ascension. The narrative of Light Language transcends mere syllables and sounds; it is an experiential form of communion that taps directly into the multidimensional nuances of consciousness.

The Essence of Light Language

Light Language doesn't abide by the linear constructs of conventional human languages. It isn't something you learn from a textbook or memorize like an earthly dialect. It's an inherently intuitive, vibrational language conveyed through tones, symbols, and multidimensional energy configurations. Some claim it originates from the Pleiadian Star System, while others propose that it's a cosmic "lingua franca" utilized across various star systems and dimensions.

While conventional languages rely on culturally derived syntax and semantics, Light Language functions through the interplay of consciousness and vibrational energy. It activates dormant DNA strands and aligns you with your higher self, serving as a direct conduit to the Universal Source. For Pleiadian Starseeds, the comprehension and use of Light Language can feel like a soulful reunion, reconnecting you with your galactic heritage and family.

Practical Uses for Starseeds

Activation and Healing

The primary use of Light Language among Starseeds is for activation and healing. Vocalizing or writing down these multi-dimensional codes can trigger an innate "remembrance," unlocking psychic abilities and enhancing spiritual ascension. For those struggling with earthly challenges, such as emotional imbalances or physical ailments, Light Language serves as a complementary form of energy healing.

Communication and Spiritual Guidance

Light Language also enables an enhanced form of telepathic communication, both with other Starseeds and with spiritual guides. It provides a direct channel to higher wisdom, bypassing the limitations of human cognition. Many Pleiadian Starseeds find it easier to connect with their Pleiadian guides or soul family using Light Language, as it resonates with their native vibrational frequencies.

Creative Manifestation

The power of Light Language extends to the realm of creative manifestation. By integrating these high-vibrational codes into meditation or ritualistic practices, you can align your intentions with the Universal Source. This facilitates the materialization of your desires, whether they are related to personal growth, relationships, or your mission on Earth.

Learning and Incorporating Light Language

Unlocking the potential of Light Language involves a deeply personal journey. While you can't "learn" it in a conventional sense, certain practices can help you tune into this frequency. Meditation is a useful starting point. During meditative sessions, allow your intuition to guide your vocalizations or hand movements. Don't be afraid to produce unfamiliar tones or doodle inexplicable symbols.

Dreamwork is another avenue for exploring Light Language. Pay close attention to symbols, sounds, or dialogues that occur in dreams. As a Starseed, your soul travels extensively during sleep, and Light Language often surfaces in these interdimensional journeys. As you become more familiar with Light Language, consider incorporating it into your healing practices, spiritual rituals, or even in your artistic pursuits. You might find that it not only enhances your personal well-being but also contributes to the collective consciousness in a meaningful way.

Summary

Light Language serves as a cosmic symphony of soul and energy, deeply integrated with the Pleiadian Starseed's journey towards spiritual enlightenment and cosmic unity. Its applications range from activation and healing to interdimensional communication and creative manifestation. As you become attuned to this extraordinary language, you'll discover new pathways to your galactic heritage, thereby fulfilling a critical aspect of your role in the Galactic Family. While Light Language might seem enigmatic and elusive, it is a natural extension of your multidimensional self, waiting to be awakened and expressed.

PART VIII: CHALLENGES AND HEALING

CHAPTER 1: EARTHLY STRUGGLES: ADJUSTING TO 3D LIFE

Introduction

Welcome to Part VIII of this expansive journey into the depths of Pleiadian Starseed wisdom. This part is focused on Challenges and Healing. Even with all the spiritual tools, psychic abilities, and deep-rooted connections to the Pleiades, adjusting to life in the third dimension can be overwhelming for a Pleiadian Starseed. This chapter will delve into the struggles you may face, providing both clarity and guidance on how to navigate this earthly existence with greater ease.

The Dissonance of Dimensions

One of the most significant challenges a Pleiadian Starseed encounters on Earth is dimensional dissonance. Accustomed to higher vibrational states of existence, the Starseed finds it challenging to navigate the density of the third dimension. In the Pleiadian star system, energetic fields are less rigid, allowing for more straightforward communication and a heightened sense of unity. On Earth, these energies are condensed, making the experience more intense and often overwhelming.

A common symptom of this dissonance is spiritual fatigue. This can manifest as a persistent emotional drain, inexplicable sadness, or a general lack of enthusiasm for life. The trick is not to resist these feelings but to understand them as part of your larger journey. Incorporating grounding techniques, such as grounding meditations or even simple walks in nature, can help recalibrate your energies and make this transition smoother. If you find yourself empathically absorbing the moods and thoughts of those around you, protective energy fields can be visualized to insulate your emotional state.

Navigating Earthly Constructs

Earthly life comes with its own set of constructs and limitations that can feel very restricting to a Pleiadian Starseed. The bureaucratic tape of human society—laws, regulations, and societal expectations—can seem overwhelming and often meaningless. These are further complicated by financial systems, political hierarchies, and cultural norms that can seem incredibly alien to someone used to the more egalitarian society of the Pleiades.

Work and professional settings can pose their own set of challenges. Pleiadian Starseeds are often drawn to helping professions or creative endeavors that allow them to make a meaningful impact. However, they can find themselves disheartened by workplace politics, rigid hierarchies, and the overemphasis on material success.

When grappling with these constructs, the key is alignment with one's inner truth. The challenge is to find a way to navigate these structures while keeping your soul's purpose intact. This may mean choosing a career that aligns with your values, even if it isn't the most financially rewarding, or setting firm boundaries that allow you to maintain your integrity within societal norms.

Relationships and Social Complexities

The intricacies of human relationships can be a complex area for Pleiadian Starseeds. While they are innately empathetic and often make for extraordinary friends and partners, the undercurrents of manipulation, ego clashes, and misunderstandings typical in earthly relationships can be hard to navigate.

Moreover, because of their heightened sensitivities, Pleiadian Starseeds might find themselves in the midst of emotional or energy vampires who drain them. Understanding the dynamics of human relationships and setting firm emotional and energetic boundaries is vital. This could mean consciously limiting time spent with individuals who drain you emotionally or finding methods to shield your energy when interacting in larger social settings.

Summary

Adjusting to life on Earth, with its dense energies and complex social systems, can be a daunting task for Pleiadian Starseeds. Challenges can range from emotional and spiritual fatigue due to dimensional dissonance, navigating perplexing societal norms, to understanding the complex realm of human relationships. However, by aligning with your inner truths and setting appropriate boundaries, you can navigate these complexities more effectively. Grounding techniques can help deal with dimensional dissonance, while a focus on alignment can help make sense of earthly constructs. Finally, a deep understanding of human relationships will assist in developing healthier interactions. These tools are not just survival mechanisms but strategies for thriving on this beautiful yet challenging planet.

CHAPTER 2: EMOTIONAL BLOCKAGES AND HOW TO HEAL THEM

Introduction

While your Pleiadian roots endow you with many unique gifts and a deep sense of spiritual connectedness, they can also make you susceptible to certain emotional challenges. Given the higher vibrational environment from which you originate, Earth's denser emotional landscape can be difficult to navigate. Here, we'll delve into some common emotional blockages experienced by Pleiadian Starseeds and offer tools for their healing.

Types of Emotional Blockages

Suppressed Emotions

Coming from a culture of open emotional exchange, Pleiadian Starseeds may find Earth's society relatively repressive when it comes to expressing feelings. This dissonance can lead to the accumulation of suppressed emotions like sadness, frustration, and even anger. The weight of these suppressed emotions can manifest as chronic physical ailments, from tension headaches to digestive issues.

Emotional Overwhelm

Pleiadians are naturally empathetic beings. While this trait can be a blessing, it can also be overwhelming when navigating an environment teeming with disparate energies and emotional states. Starseeds may sometimes experience emotional overload, making it difficult to distinguish their feelings from those around them.

Fear of Rejection

Being a Starseed means you are inherently different in various ways, which might make you sensitive to the possibility of social rejection. Even though your mission is noble and your qualities are rare, the fear of not being accepted can be paralyzing and lead to emotional stagnation.

Healing Strategies

Emotional Release Techniques

There are multiple ways to channel your suppressed emotions constructively:

1. **Journaling**: Writing down what you feel can offer a release valve for your suppressed emotions and also offer insights into the root causes.
2. **Physical Exercise**: Physical activities like running, yoga, or even dancing can help release pent-up energy.
3. **Artistic Expression**: For those inclined, painting, singing, or any form of artistic expression can serve as

an emotional outlet.

Energy Clearing Practices

Being overwhelmed by external energies calls for regular energetic clearing:

1. **Meditation**: A focused meditation practice can not only still the mind but also help you in clearing your emotional and energetic body.
2. **Energy Healing**: Modalities like Reiki, or Pleiadian lightwork, can be exceptionally beneficial.

Facing Your Fears

Acknowledging the fear of rejection or any other fears you have is the first step in overcoming them. Try to understand where these fears stem from and how they have shaped your behavior and choices. Strategies include affirmations, and if necessary, seeking help from therapists or counselors specialized in spiritual or existential concerns.

The Pleiadian Approach to Emotional Well-being

In Pleiadian cultures, emotional well-being is often achieved through community and connection. Emotional exchange is considered not just therapeutic but sacred. There is no shame in seeking help, be it from family, friends, or healers. Emotions are viewed as a form of energy, meant to flow rather than be stifled. Bringing some of these perspectives into your earthly experience can be invaluable.

Summary

Emotional blockages can be a significant impediment in your life, more so when you are attuned to higher frequencies and greater emotional depth. Understanding the types of blockages and knowing how to heal them can lead to a more fulfilling and less stressful life. Strategies range from emotional release techniques and energy clearing practices to facing your fears head-on. Adopting the Pleiadian perspective of viewing emotions as sacred can shift your mindset and facilitate healing at a profound level.

CHAPTER 3: THE ROLE OF EGO: LESSONS AND LEARNING

Introduction

As a Pleiadian Starseed, you're likely attuned to higher frequencies and possess an innate understanding of universal love and unity. However, life on Earth exposes you to a variety of experiences and lessons that can be challenging, not least of which is the human ego. This chapter delves into the intricacies of the ego from a Pleiadian perspective, offering wisdom on how to harmonize this element of the human psyche with your galactic identity.

Understanding the Ego in Human and Pleiadian Contexts

In the human experience, the ego is often understood as a construct of self-identity, closely tied to self-esteem, personal boundaries, and ambition. While it can be a driving force for personal growth and achievement, it also has the potential to isolate individuals by promoting a sense of separation or superiority.

In Pleiadian philosophy, the ego is not vilified; rather, it is seen as a necessary component of the learning journey. The ego, in this context, is a manifestation of the 3D self, which exists to help you navigate the material world. In Pleiadian realms, where telepathic communication is prevalent and the collective consciousness is more integrated, the ego doesn't function in the same way. However, understanding the ego from both Earthly and Pleiadian perspectives can offer valuable insights into managing it effectively.

Ego-Driven Emotional Blockages and Galactic Awareness

Many emotional blockages can be attributed to an overactive ego. Feelings of superiority, jealousy, or extreme self-criticism can distort your view of yourself and others. These emotions can become even more convoluted when viewed through the lens of being a Starseed. You might feel an egotistical pride about your Pleiadian heritage or, conversely, a heavy burden of responsibility.

Recognizing these tendencies is the first step in disentangling ego-driven blockages. The Pleiadian approach involves raising your awareness to include your multi-dimensional self, allowing a balancing and harmonization between ego-driven impulses and soul-driven wisdom. Once you understand that the ego is a tool rather than the essence of your being, you can use it to navigate the material world while being guided by the higher wisdom of your galactic self.

Pleiadian Techniques for Ego Management

Here are some practices inspired by Pleiadian philosophy for managing the ego:

- **Observational Meditation**: Sit quietly and observe your thoughts without judgment. Note any thoughts that seem rooted in ego such as comparison, envy, or self-aggrandizement. Merely observing these thoughts can diminish their emotional charge.

- **Galactic Grounding**: Engage in grounding exercises, but with a twist. Visualize your grounding cord extending to the core of Earth while another cord extends toward the Pleiades. Feel the balance between Earthly and cosmic energies.
- **Heart-Centered Dialogue**: When engaged in a conversation, try to speak from your heart rather than your ego. Visualize a warm, golden light in your heart chakra and imagine your words flowing from this space. This can create an atmosphere of genuine exchange, reducing the room for egoic distortion.

Summary

The ego can be a complex and challenging aspect of human life, particularly for Pleiadian Starseeds who are navigating both Earthly and galactic identities. Understanding the role of ego in the human psyche and learning how to manage it can significantly assist in your emotional and spiritual development. Techniques like observational meditation, galactic grounding, and heart-centered dialogue can help in balancing ego-driven impulses with the wisdom of your multi-dimensional, galactic self. By addressing the ego with awareness and compassion, you can harmonize it with your higher self, thereby enriching both your Earthly experience and your galactic journey.

CHAPTER 4: BALANCING DUAL IDENTITIES

Introduction

Navigating one's identity is an intricate process in the human experience, often fraught with questions, uncertainties, and discoveries. For Pleiadian Starseeds, the complexity multiplies, given the duality of existing as both a human and a galactic entity. This chapter delves into the art of balancing these dual identities, addressing the cognitive, emotional, and spiritual aspects involved.

The Cognitive Aspect: Bridging Two Worlds Through Thought

Starseeds inherently operate from a dichotomy of perspectives. They possess an earthly consciousness that is deeply rooted in the tangible, the immediate, and the material, while also sustaining a higher vibrational consciousness resonating with Pleiadian wisdom and cosmic connectivity. The challenge here is to bring coherence between these two cognitive dimensions. How can you rationalize your earthly struggles when your higher self operates from a plane of elevated understanding and unconditional love?

1. **Acknowledge the Duality**: Pretending one aspect of

your identity doesn't exist will not make it go away; it will only create an internal imbalance.

2. **Integrate, Don't Isolate**: When your earthly mind puzzles over a problem, invite your higher self into the contemplative space. Look at challenges from both a terrestrial and a celestial viewpoint.

3. **Prioritize Fluidity over Rigidity**: The balance between your dual identities is not a static state but a dynamic equilibrium. A rigid mental structure that confines your Pleiadian identity to a set of predetermined thoughts or rules will only hinder the flow of energy between your dual identities.

The Emotional Aspect: Harmonizing Earthly and Cosmic Emotions

Balancing dual identities also requires managing a complicated emotional tapestry. Emotions such as fear, sadness, or anger that are often seen as "negative" within earthly contexts might not have an equivalent in the Pleiadian emotional spectrum, which tends to operate on frequencies of unconditional love and higher wisdom.

1. **Embrace Emotional Complexity**: Accept that you will feel a broad spectrum of emotions, some of which are exclusively earthly, and others that are celestial.

2. **Transmute Emotions**: Use techniques like emotional alchemy, wherein you actively transform lower-vibrational emotions into higher ones. For example, transmute anger into compassion or fear into courage by consciously invoking your higher Pleiadian wisdom.

3. **Seek Emotional Integration**: Always aim for an integrated emotional response that combines your

human and Pleiadian identities. When encountering a challenge, respond with both earthly prudence and cosmic wisdom.

The Spiritual Aspect: Uniting Two Souls in One Existence

A significant part of balancing dual identities lies in harmonizing your earthly soul with your Pleiadian spirit. Your human soul gains experiences, learns karmic lessons, and undergoes spiritual evolution, while your Pleiadian spirit already resonates at a higher level of wisdom and cosmic understanding.

1. **Holistic Spiritual Practices**: Utilize practices that serve both aspects of your being. For instance, meditation techniques that focus on grounding can be combined with lightwork that connects to higher realms.
2. **Soul-Spirit Dialogue**: Maintain an internal dialogue between your earthly soul and Pleiadian spirit. This could be achieved through journaling, deep meditation, or even dream work where you request guidance from both.
3. **Conscious Coexistence**: Finally, consciously allow both your soul and spirit to coexist and co-lead in your life. The human aspect of you is not inferior; it merely offers a different set of experiences and lessons.

Summary

Balancing dual identities is not about choosing one over the other, or about creating a synthesized, hybrid identity that is somehow less than either of its parts. It's about acknowledging, respecting, and integrating both identities in a harmonious way that allows for growth, learning, and a richer, more fulfilling existence. Through cognitive reconciliation, emotional harmonization, and spiritual unification, Pleiadian Starseeds can achieve a balanced state of being that honors the fullness of their complex identity.

CHAPTER 5: BUILDING RESILIENCE: STRATEGIES FOR DIFFICULT TIMES

Introduction

Life on Earth can be a whirlwind of experiences, both euphoric and challenging. The intricacies of third-dimensional existence often present unique struggles for Pleiadian Starseeds, who sometimes find it difficult to adapt to the density and limitations of Earthly life. How does one build resilience to weather these challenges while maintaining alignment with their higher selves and galactic mission? In this chapter, we will delve into various strategies tailored for Pleiadian Starseeds to fortify themselves mentally, emotionally, and spiritually in the face of adversities.

Cultivating Emotional Resilience

Emotional resilience is not just the absence of distress but the ability to bounce back from it. Emotional highs and lows are part and parcel of earthly life, but they can be especially overwhelming for Pleiadian Starseeds who often possess a heightened emotional sensitivity.

Harness the Power of Perspective

One key to emotional resilience lies in your perspective. View your challenges not as obstacles but as lessons in disguise. Your earthly experiences, no matter how taxing, offer invaluable opportunities for soul evolution. By recognizing the wisdom embedded within your struggles, you can transmute emotional turbulence into enlightening insight.

Emotional Catharsis: Channel and Release

Holding onto negative emotions can create blockages in your energy field. Practices such as journaling, expressive arts, or even meditative visualization can be transformative. Through these practices, you can identify, understand, and release the emotional energy that no longer serves you, making room for healing and growth.

Building Mental Resilience

Mental resilience goes hand-in-hand with emotional resilience but focuses more on your thought patterns and cognitive behaviors. Pleiadian wisdom offers unique approaches to cultivate a robust mental framework.

Mindfulness and Present Moment Awareness

Mindfulness is the practice of grounding your awareness into the present moment, thereby short-circuiting looping thought patterns and anxiety about the future or the past. By being fully present, you align more closely with your higher self, which exists beyond the constraints of time and space. Mindfulness techniques can range from breath awareness to full-fledged meditation.

Cognitive Reframing: Mastering Your Mindset

Your thoughts have a potent influence on your reality. Cognitive reframing is the art of deliberately changing your mental framework to interpret experiences in a way that serves you better. For instance, instead of saying, "Why does this always happen to me?" you could reframe it as, "What can I learn from this experience?" This shift places you in a position of empowerment, allowing for transformative experiences.

Strengthening Spiritual Resilience

The final and perhaps the most vital component of resilience is spiritual resilience—your ability to maintain alignment with your higher self and purpose, especially when facing hardships.

Grounding Techniques

Pleiadian Starseeds often struggle with grounding because their energies are naturally attuned to higher dimensions. However, grounding is essential for spiritual resilience. Simple practices like walking barefoot on the Earth, engaging with nature, or using grounding crystals can create an energetic link to Earth, which in turn provides a stabilizing effect on your spiritual being.

Community and Soul Family

Never underestimate the power of community in building resilience. Your soul family, both earthly and galactic, serve as pillars of support and mirrors for self-reflection. Engage with communities that resonate with you, be it Pleiadian-focused groups or broader spiritual communities. Shared wisdom and collective energy can substantially bolster your spiritual resilience.

Summary

Building resilience is not a one-off task but an ongoing process, requiring consistent effort and awareness. Emotional resilience can be cultivated by altering your perspective and through emotional catharsis. Mental resilience is built through mindfulness and cognitive reframing, while spiritual resilience is strengthened through grounding techniques and fostering community connections. By integrating these diverse yet interconnected strategies, Pleiadian Starseeds can build a comprehensive resilience system that empowers them to navigate the challenges of earthly life while remaining anchored to their higher purpose.

PART IX: WORKING WITH SPIRIT GUIDES

CHAPTER 1: WHO ARE SPIRIT GUIDES?

Introduction

As you embark on your journey toward understanding your role within the Galactic Family, the concept of Spirit Guides becomes increasingly essential. These ethereal beings play a pivotal role in your spiritual development, offering guidance, wisdom, and sometimes direct intervention in your Earthly life. This chapter aims to demystify the notion of Spirit Guides within the context of Pleiadian Starseeds, explaining their characteristics, roles, and the dynamic ways in which they interact with you.

The Nature of Spirit Guides

In Pleiadian cosmology, Spirit Guides are often referred to as "Light Mentors," echoing their role as teachers and guides who assist you on your journey of self-discovery and spiritual growth. These Light Mentors are multidimensional beings with an elevated level of consciousness, existing in frequencies that are often beyond the range of ordinary human perception. They have transcended the limitations of physical existence and are aligned with the principles of unconditional love, wisdom, and cosmic law.

Spirit Guides come from various dimensions and cosmic origins. While some may have Pleiadian roots, others could belong to different star systems or even other dimensions entirely. They may present themselves in various forms—such as light patterns, human or animal figures, or ethereal shapes—depending on the level of consciousness of the individual they are assisting and the specific lessons that need to be imparted.

Roles and Responsibilities

The Light Mentors have various roles that generally revolve around steering you toward your highest potential. They may assist in a variety of ways, such as:

- **Navigational Guidance:** Spirit Guides can offer insights into choices you may need to make, pointing you toward opportunities for growth, though they will always honor your free will.
- **Emotional Support:** During times of emotional turmoil, the calming energies of your Spirit Guides can offer a sense of peace and clarity. They may impart intuitive nudges or send synchronicities your way to let you know you're not alone.
- **Spiritual Awakening:** Light Mentors often facilitate spiritual experiences that can catalyze your awakening, pushing you to question your existential realities and dig deeper into the cosmic aspects of your being.

However, it is vital to note that despite their roles in guiding and assisting you, they will not interfere with your life lessons or karmic contracts. The key principle here is that of free will; your Spirit Guides will never compel you to take a specific action but instead present options and perspectives for you to consider.

Establishing the Connection

One of the most common questions Starseeds have is how to effectively connect with their Spirit Guides. The answer lies in the frequency and the quality of one's intention. Spirit Guides operate on higher frequency bands; thus, raising your vibration through practices such as meditation, energy work, and ethical living can make the communicative pathways clearer. Regularly asking for guidance and being open to receiving messages in various forms—such as dreams, intuition, or even physical signs—can solidify this connection over time.

The relationship with your Spirit Guides is a two-way street. While they are ready to offer their wisdom, it is equally crucial for you to be open, receptive, and proactive in seeking their guidance. Over time, this relationship can develop into a deeply enriching and symbiotic partnership that significantly amplifies your spiritual journey.

Summary

The concept of Spirit Guides or Light Mentors is a cornerstone in the life of a Pleiadian Starseed, serving as invaluable allies on your spiritual journey. Their multi-dimensional nature, rooted in higher levels of consciousness, allows them to offer a unique perspective that can be immensely beneficial in your Earthly life. By understanding their roles, respecting the boundaries of free will, and making a conscious effort to connect, you can forge a profound relationship with these ethereal beings, enriching both your Earthly experience and your broader cosmic journey.

CHAPTER 2: CONTACTING YOUR PLEIADIAN GUIDES

Introduction

Having understood the concept and roles of spirit guides, as explored in the previous chapter, it's crucial to delve into the specifics of establishing contact with your Pleiadian spirit guides. This chapter serves as a primer for those who wish to strengthen their connection to the Pleiadian realm, offering meticulous guidance and practices for achieving a more profound spiritual link. We will discuss multiple methodologies, ranging from meditative techniques to mystical rituals, that can help facilitate this vital connection.

Meditative Techniques

Meditation is one of the most direct ways to reach out to your Pleiadian guides. The tranquility and clarity achieved through meditation can offer a conducive environment for spiritual interaction.

1. **Focused Attention Meditation**: Sit comfortably in a quiet space, close your eyes, and focus on your breath. Gradually, let your mind drift to the Pleiadian star system, imagining its brilliant light. As you breathe in,

visualize this light flowing into you. As you exhale, let go of earthly tensions. Maintain this focus and silently request contact from your Pleiadian guides.

2. **Guided Meditation**: There are specialized Pleiadian guided meditations available that are designed to connect you to Pleiadian energy. These meditations often involve visualizations of Pleiadian landscapes or meeting with Pleiadian beings in ethereal spaces. The guide's voice, often imbued with energetic frequencies, can facilitate the connection.

3. **Mantra Meditation**: Pleiadian mantras can serve as another tool. Repeating a specific Pleiadian mantra, either vocally or mentally, can attract the energies of your Pleiadian guides, making it easier for them to reach you.

Mystical Rituals

While meditative practices appeal to the individual's inner world, mystical rituals engage with the external environment to manifest spiritual connections.

1. **Sacred Geometry**: Drawing Pleiadian symbols or sacred geometry on paper or in the air can activate specific energies. These symbols act like keys to the Pleiadian realm and can open channels of communication when used correctly.

2. **Crystal Grids**: The use of Pleiadian-associated crystals like Moldavite, Lapis Lazuli, or Clear Quartz in a specific geometric pattern can amplify your intent to contact Pleiadian guides. The grid acts as an energetic focal point, accumulating energies conducive for contact.

3. **Pleiadian Lightwork**: This involves complex

rituals that may require advanced knowledge in esoteric principles. Usually conducted under certain astrological configurations, Pleiadian lightwork involves chants, invocations, and the use of various sacred objects to create a potent energetic environment.

Ethical Considerations

In your quest to connect with your Pleiadian guides, it's vital to approach the practice with integrity and respect. Unethical practices like attempting to bind or control these higher beings, or using their guidance for harmful purposes, are strongly discouraged. Pleiadian entities are beings of light and love; they respect free will and expect the same in return. Maintaining an ethical stance not only respects these beings but also ensures that your spiritual journey is beneficial to all involved.

Summary

In summary, the chapter aims to provide a detailed, yet caring guide on multiple methods to establish contact with your Pleiadian guides. Whether you choose to engage through meditation or more external mystical rituals, the intent and focus are crucial elements. It is imperative to combine this search for external wisdom with an ethical and respectful approach. As you make contact with your Pleiadian guides, remember that you are opening a channel of communication with highly evolved beings who can provide you not only with guidance but also offer a deeper understanding of your role in the Galactic Family. This contact serves to enhance your spiritual journey, provided it is embarked upon with earnestness and integrity.

CHAPTER 3: CHANNELING MESSAGES

Introduction

Channeling messages from Pleiadian spirit guides is an intriguing and enlightening facet of Pleiadian spirituality. It allows you a personal connection with celestial wisdom and guidance tailored to your current state and the specific challenges you might be facing. Whether you seek to gain higher insights, resolve karmic issues, or deepen your understanding of your purpose as a Pleiadian starseed, channeling messages is a rewarding endeavor. However, channeling isn't just a matter of turning on a switch; it involves meticulous preparation and a balanced mental state. This chapter aims to guide you through the processes and techniques necessary for successful channeling.

Mental and Emotional Preparation

Setting the Intention

The first step in channeling is to set a clear intention. What are you hoping to achieve through this channeling session? It could be as simple as seeking general guidance, or as specific as asking for insight into a particular life event. Formulate your questions or intentions in your mind and perhaps even voice them aloud or write them down.

Creating a Sacred Space

Creating a dedicated space for channeling helps focus your energy and shields you from external influences. This space should be clean, quiet, and free from disturbances. You may use candles, incense, or crystals to help set the ambiance and raise the vibration of the space. While these are not mandatory, they can enhance your focus and receptivity.

Emotional Balance

Your emotional state plays a crucial role in the channeling process. Negative emotions like fear, doubt, or skepticism can cloud the channel and interfere with the clarity of the messages. Therefore, it's essential to calm your mind and center your emotions before initiating the channeling session. Techniques such as deep breathing, meditation, or grounding exercises can help you achieve a balanced emotional state.

Techniques for Channeling Messages

Tuning In

Imagine a stream of light connecting you from your crown chakra at the top of your head to the Pleiadian guides. Visualize this stream becoming brighter and stronger as you concentrate. This is your connection, your spiritual broadband if you will, linking you to higher dimensions. Some people find that their body starts to tingle, or they experience a lightness as they tune in. These are generally good signs that you are successfully tuning into the higher vibrational frequencies.

Receiving and Interpreting Messages

Messages from Pleiadian guides can come in various forms. Some people hear them as thoughts, distinct from their thinking process. Others see images or even get a 'knowing' sense, a sudden and clear understanding of what is being communicated. When you receive these messages, it's crucial to not overanalyze them in the moment. Instead, maintain your receptive state and let the impressions flow.

Documenting the Session

As messages can sometimes be fleeting or layered with complex symbolism, it is advisable to document the session. You can either write down what you're experiencing in real-time or record it for later review. Revisiting these documented messages can offer new insights and even reveal information that was not initially understood.

Troubleshooting and Fine-Tuning

Handling Distractions

It's normal to get distracted, especially if you're new to channeling. If this happens, don't get frustrated. Simply acknowledge the distraction and bring your focus back to the channel. Sometimes these distractions are a form of resistance that needs to be worked through and understood.

Fine-Tuning the Connection

With practice, you'll notice that your ability to channel messages becomes more refined. You'll learn to distinguish between the subtleties of different energetic frequencies and will become more adept at focusing on the specific guide or source you wish to channel. Just like any other skill, practice makes perfect.

Summary

Channeling messages from your Pleiadian guides offers invaluable insights into your journey as a starseed. It's a skill that requires both emotional balance and mental focus, but the rewards are immeasurable. From setting a clear intention and creating a sacred space to tuning in and receiving messages, each step is crucial for a successful channeling session. With regular practice, you'll become more proficient, and the messages you channel will gain in clarity and depth. Remember, channeling is not merely a method to receive information but a path that leads you closer to your higher self and your Pleiadian lineage.

CHAPTER 4: ENHANCING YOUR PSYCHIC ABILITIES

Introduction

After exploring the realm of spirit guides and channeling messages, it's time to delve deeper into the less tangible but equally powerful aspect of your spiritual journey—enhancing your psychic abilities. The Pleiadian approach to psychic growth is holistic, integrating the physical, emotional, and spiritual dimensions of existence. This chapter aims to provide a comprehensive and caring guide to nurturing these abilities, allowing you to experience an enriched interaction with both your earthly and galactic environments.

The Pleiadian Framework for Psychic Enhancement

The Pleiadian perspective on psychic abilities is interwoven with their understanding of multi-dimensionality and interconnectedness. It is believed that all beings, Pleiadian or otherwise, possess latent psychic abilities, but these skills are often dormant due to various factors like societal conditioning, emotional blockages, or simply a lack of awareness. The goal is to 'unlock' these capabilities, not just for personal enrichment but also for the collective good.

1. **Awareness and Acceptance:** The first step in any psychic journey is the acknowledgement that you possess these abilities. Pleiadians emphasize the need for cultivating a personal sense of awareness that cuts through societal skepticism or any personal doubts.

2. **Alignment with Higher Self:** The Higher Self is considered the repository of immense wisdom and psychic capabilities. Aligning with it often involves deep meditation, spiritual practices, and sometimes guidance from spiritual mentors or guides.

3. **Application:** Pleiadians advocate the practical application of psychic skills as a means of reinforcing them. This can range from intuitive decision-making to more advanced practices like energy healing and telepathy.

Techniques for Psychic Development

Pleiadians employ a myriad of techniques for psychic development, but we'll focus on three core practices that are adaptable and effective across various contexts:

1. **Vibrational Tuning:** In this practice, you use meditation and conscious thought to raise your vibrational frequency. Higher vibrations are believed to facilitate a clearer and more potent psychic perception. You may employ tools like crystals, which we discussed in an earlier chapter, to amplify this process.

2. **Symbolic Interpretation:** Pleiadians frequently use symbols as a language that transcends the spoken word. This technique involves meditation upon specific symbols, such as geometric shapes or glyphs, that can activate or amplify psychic faculties. The visualization of these symbols, particularly during

meditative states, has the potential to unlock deeper layers of your subconscious and supercharge your psychic abilities.

3. **Energetic Feedback Loop:** This is an advanced technique where you consciously send and receive energy with your environment or another individual. The purpose is to hone your abilities to manipulate and interpret psychic energy. It's much like a conversation but on an energetic level.

Balancing and Grounding

When developing psychic abilities, the Pleiadians stress the importance of balancing and grounding these new skills. An ungrounded psychic awakening can lead to emotional volatility and even physical symptoms. Pleiadians recommend grounding techniques like connecting with nature, channeling excess energy into the Earth, and regular practices that focus on the lower chakras to maintain a balanced energetic profile.

To balance the awakening process, it's also crucial to embrace ethical considerations, which keep your psychic interactions respectful and beneficial for all involved. This involves using your abilities responsibly and with the intention of positive change or understanding, rather than for manipulative or self-serving purposes.

Summary

In the Pleiadian viewpoint, psychic abilities are not exclusive gifts but rather innate aspects of our multidimensional selves waiting to be awakened. By adopting a Pleiadian framework that integrates awareness, alignment with the Higher Self, and practical application, you set the stage for a purposeful and ethically grounded psychic evolution. The key techniques of vibrational tuning, symbolic interpretation, and the energetic feedback loop can significantly aid in this transformative journey. Balancing and grounding your newfound abilities are equally essential, ensuring that you're both ethically and energetically aligned in your psychic practices. These teachings serve as not just tools for personal growth but as conduits for contributing positively to the collective consciousness, aligning with the Pleiadian vision of unity and mutual evolution.

CHAPTER 5: SACRED SITES: EARTHLY CONNECTIONS TO PLEIADIAN ENERGIES

Introduction

The relationship between earthly locations and Pleiadian energies is a concept that has fascinated many a Starseed and spiritual seeker. Understanding the connection can unlock powerful insights and catalyze deeper spiritual experiences. This chapter delves into the significance of these sacred sites, how they are energetically connected to Pleiadian energies, and how you can benefit from visiting or tuning into these powerful locations.

What Makes a Site Sacred?

Sacred sites are not just historical landmarks or natural wonders. They are, in essence, energetic vortices where the Earth's own magnetic fields intersect with cosmic energies in a unique and powerful way. Pleiadian Starseeds often find themselves inexplicably drawn to these sites, whether it's the Great Pyramids of Giza, the mysterious stone circles of Stonehenge, or the spiritual depths of Mount Shasta. The subtle energies that permeate these places resonate with the Pleiadian frequency, making them portals for higher dimensional experiences.

It's not just about physical location; sacred sites also often become focal points for accumulated wisdom, rituals, and spiritual practices of the local culture. When these human activities synchronize with the natural energies of the site, the result can be an exponentially potent energetic environment. Pleiadian energies, which are inherently attuned to higher dimensions of consciousness, can then interact more fluidly with these sites, further amplifying their spiritual significance.

Recognizing Pleiadian Energies at Sacred Sites

Starseeds and seekers might wonder how to recognize or confirm Pleiadian energies at a sacred site. While scientific instrumentation to quantify these subtle energies is still in nascent stages, our own intuitive faculties are remarkable sensors for such phenomena. Here are some experiential cues:

- **Deep Emotional Resonance**: You may feel an overwhelming sense of 'coming home' or belonging. There might be a profound emotional release or realization.
- **Enhanced Psychic Abilities**: Your intuitive or psychic faculties might be significantly heightened. This can manifest as clearer visions, acute telepathic communication, or enhanced empathy.
- **Synchronicities**: Pay attention to synchronicities or 'meaningful coincidences' that occur around your visit. These might be messages from Pleiadian guides or your higher self signaling your alignment with the energy of the site.

- **Physical Sensations**: You may experience tingling in your chakras, especially your crown, third-eye, and heart chakras. Some people describe this as a 'buzzing' sensation that engulfs them while they are at the site.

Engaging with Pleiadian Energies at Sacred Sites

Simply being at a sacred site can be a transformative experience, but actively engaging with its energies can be even more rewarding. Here's how you can connect more deeply:

- **Meditation**: Use focused meditation techniques to tap into the Pleiadian frequencies. Visualize a beam of Pleiadian light descending into the site and entering your body, harmonizing with your energetic field.
- **Chanting and Light Language**: Employ sacred sounds, mantras, or light language to resonate with the energy frequencies of the site. The vibrational qualities of these sounds can activate latent codes within you.
- **Rituals and Ceremonies**: Engage in rituals or ceremonies that align with your intentions and the energies of the site. Whether it's a moon ritual, offering crystals, or performing a sacred dance, make sure it comes from a place of respect for both the land and the traditions associated with it.
- **Journaling**: Keep a journal to document your experiences, insights, and any messages that might come through. Writing aids in integrating these profound experiences into your conscious understanding.

Summary

Sacred sites provide a physical focal point where Pleiadian energies intersect with Earth's own energetic grid. Understanding and engaging with these unique sites can be a rewarding aspect of your spiritual journey as a Pleiadian Starseed. Recognizing the energetic signatures and actively meditating or performing rituals can amplify your connection, not just to the Pleiades but to your higher self and the intricate web of consciousness that binds the universe. Whether you find yourself walking the ley lines of ancient sites or communing with nature in a secluded grove, remember that you are a part of this grand cosmic interplay, ever-connected, ever-guided, and eternally loved.

PART X: PLEIADIAN WISDOM FOR EARTHLY LIFE

CHAPTER 1: SUSTAINABLE LIVING: A PLEIADIAN APPROACH

In this chapter, we explore the Pleiadian philosophy on sustainable living, a topic of growing importance given the current challenges facing Earth. Pleiadian wisdom extends far beyond spirituality and psychic abilities; it also provides valuable insights into the manner in which we can harmoniously coexist with our planet. Let's delve into the key tenets that guide the Pleiadian approach to sustainability.

Harmony with Nature

At the core of Pleiadian sustainability practices is a deep-rooted respect for Nature. In Pleiadian societies, the natural world isn't just a resource to be used; it's a living entity to be honored. This belief system creates a symbiotic relationship between Pleiadians and their environment. Every element, from the water to the flora and fauna, is revered as an intricate part of the greater cosmic puzzle.

Advanced technologies in Pleiadian realms are developed with this philosophy in mind. Unlike Earth, where technology often poses a threat to the environment, Pleiadian innovation is geared towards minimizing ecological footprints. For example, instead of burning fossil fuels, Pleiadians use renewable energy sources that harness cosmic currents and natural magnetic fields. The key takeaway here is that technological advancement and environmental conservation are not mutually exclusive but can exist in harmony.

Circular Economy and Resource Sharing

The economic systems in Pleiadian societies function on a radically different premise than the predominantly linear systems of Earth. Pleiadians operate on what could be best described as a "circular economy." In this system, products are designed to last, and once they reach the end of their life cycle, they are either refurbished or disassembled for parts, which are then recycled into new products. This is in stark contrast to the "use and discard" model prevalent in many Earth societies.

Resource sharing is another cornerstone of Pleiadian sustainability. Rather than individual ownership, resources and goods are often community-owned. This encourages responsible utilization and minimizes waste. Shared ownership also fosters a sense of community and mutual respect among Pleiadians, strengthening social fabric and collective responsibility.

Mindful Consumption

Pleiadians place immense value on mindful consumption—whether it be food, material goods, or even information. In Pleiadian cultures, the act of consuming is not merely functional; it's an exercise in consciousness. Before consuming anything, Pleiadians are taught to contemplate its origin, its impact on their well-being, and the environmental toll of its production.

Food, for instance, is often grown through advanced forms of permaculture that enrich the soil rather than deplete it. And when it comes to material goods, emphasis is placed on quality over quantity, encouraging the use of goods that are made to last and can be recycled or reused.

Summary

The Pleiadian approach to sustainability offers a deeply resonant alternative to how Earth currently interacts with its environment. Rooted in a philosophy of harmony with nature, the Pleiadian model champions technological innovation that complements rather than exploits the Earth. Through a circular economy and shared resources, Pleiadians minimize waste and encourage responsible use. Finally, their practice of mindful consumption serves as a reminder that sustainability is not just an external practice but also an internal mindset.

While adopting these practices wholesale may not be immediately feasible for Earth, understanding these tenets can provide us with invaluable insights. They offer innovative pathways for those who aim for a more sustainable, harmonious existence—guiding principles that could serve us well as we navigate the pressing environmental challenges of our times.

CHAPTER 2: PLEIADIAN WISDOM ON LOVE AND RELATIONSHIPS

Introduction

Love and relationships are universally complex yet profoundly significant aspects of life, shaping our experiences and influencing our well-being on multiple dimensions. For Pleiadian Starseeds, the concept of love goes beyond earthly understanding. It serves as a complex intersection of spiritual connection, energetic resonance, and evolutionary growth. This chapter delves into Pleiadian perspectives on love and relationships, illuminating how these advanced beings conceptualize and live out these deeply essential life experiences.

The Nature of Love in Pleiadian Consciousness

In Pleiadian consciousness, love is not merely an emotion; it's a complex vibrational field that permeates the universe. It serves as a linking mechanism that binds not just individuals, but communities, star systems, and even dimensions. For Pleiadians, love is the epitome of universal language, an omnipresent force that aligns will, intention, and action.

There's an inherent recognition among Pleiadians that love is both a personal and collective experience. While love can manifest in the passionate union between two souls, it also expresses itself in broader ethical and social constructs like compassion, mutual respect, and altruism. In Pleiadian societies, love is a pervasive atmosphere where beings freely express their emotions without the constraints of judgement or societal expectations. The absence of these constraints allows for a more profound exploration and experience of love, one rooted in genuine understanding and acceptance.

Energetic Resonance and Relationships

Another crucial aspect of Pleiadian love is the focus on energetic resonance. In human terms, this would be akin to "chemistry," but for Pleiadians, it goes much deeper. When two Pleiadian beings resonate at similar frequencies, the interaction is not just emotional or physical; it's energetically synergistic. This resonance amplifies the individuals' vibrational frequencies, which not only deepens the love experience but also fosters spiritual growth for both parties involved.

Energetic resonance is considered a valuable marker for the suitability and potential longevity of relationships. Pleiadian partnerships often involve in-depth energetic assessments, somewhat like a harmonization process, to ensure that both parties will be enriched by the union rather than hindered. This doesn't mean that all Pleiadian relationships are "perfect" or without challenges. Still, the challenges are viewed as opportunities for growth and deeper resonance, rather than stumbling blocks.

Balancing Individuality and Union

In Pleiadian relationships, there's a significant emphasis on balancing the individual growth of each being with the collective evolution of the relationship. Unlike many earthly relationships where individual identities may sometimes get eclipsed by the relationship, Pleiadians view individuality as sacrosanct. The premise is that two strong, individual souls contribute more effectively to the collective consciousness when they are in a balanced and loving relationship.

This principle manifests in various practices and relationship models that are designed to foster individual growth. For instance, it's common in Pleiadian relationships to have periods of separation where each individual embarks on personal quests for knowledge, spiritual growth, or other forms of self-advancement. These periods are not considered threats to the relationship but rather enriching interludes that contribute to the overall health and vibrancy of the union.

Summary

Pleiadian perspectives on love and relationships offer profound insights that can be transformative when applied to earthly life. Their advanced understanding that love is a multi-dimensional force, the importance they place on energetic resonance, and their emphasis on balancing individual and collective growth within relationships present a holistic model that stands in marked contrast to many human paradigms of love. For Pleiadian Starseeds and those intrigued by Pleiadian wisdom, these insights serve as enlightening guidelines that can elevate your understanding and experience of one of life's most potent and mysterious forces: love.

CHAPTER 3: CAREER AND LIFE PURPOSE: ALIGNING WITH YOUR GALACTIC MISSION

In the grand design of the cosmos, every soul has a unique purpose that contributes to the expansion of collective consciousness. As a Pleiadian Starseed, your vocation on Earth might feel like a challenging puzzle, often causing you to question how you can serve both your Earthly responsibilities and your higher, galactic commitments. This chapter aims to offer Pleiadian wisdom to help you gain insight into your career and life purpose, emphasizing how you can cohesively integrate your Earthly and cosmic roles.

The Concept of Vocation in Pleiadian Philosophy

In Pleiadian understanding, your vocation isn't merely an occupation but an orchestration of your soul's essence into practical action. Pleiadians place tremendous value on personal development, the exploration of one's inherent skills, and the act of purposeful contribution. Work isn't seen as a means to an end, such as financial stability, but as a way to manifest your soul's purpose and to contribute positively to the collective.

Careers in Pleiadian societies are therefore often less rigid and more fluid than what you may be accustomed to on Earth. The emphasis is on cooperation rather than competition, where members intuitively know and embrace their roles for the higher good. This philosophy encourages you to question the Earthly paradigms you've been brought up with, such as the struggle for status, monetary success, or recognition. Instead, Pleiadians guide you toward a perspective of interconnectedness, advocating that your work should be a seamless blend of your skills, passion, and the needs of the community, both local and galactic.

Aligning Career Choices with Your Soul Contract

You may be wondering how you can recognize a career path that aligns with your cosmic mission. To grasp this, it's beneficial to understand your soul contract, an ethereal document so to speak, that outlines the major life experiences and lessons your soul chose to go through in its current incarnation. Your soul contract encapsulates not just what you will do, but what you will learn, whom you will interact with, and how you will grow. By using techniques such as meditation, introspective journaling, and intuitive readings, you can gain a clearer understanding of your soul contract and thereby realize how your Earthly career can serve your higher purpose.

For Pleiadian Starseeds, career choices that involve healing, teaching, and fostering community are often most fulfilling. These vocations naturally resonate with Pleiadian virtues and allow you to seamlessly align your Earthly responsibilities with your higher, cosmic goals. For instance, if your inherent gift is in energy healing, a career in alternative medicine or therapeutic arts could serve as a powerful platform. Those with keen diplomatic skills might find immense satisfaction in conflict-resolution or social justice work. Remember, the point isn't just to find a job but to manifest your soul's essence in a meaningful way.

The Importance of Flexibility and Adaptation

It's crucial to understand that your career and life path may undergo several changes or phases. This is not indicative of inconsistency, but rather a reflection of your soul's evolving needs and lessons. Pleiadians encourage you to embrace change with open arms, viewing it as an opportunity for growth, not a setback. Periods of uncertainty are often veiled invitations from the universe, asking you to reassess, realign, and rediscover your purpose. Adaptability, therefore, becomes an invaluable asset.

Moreover, your galactic family is always ready to offer guidance and synchronicities to help you navigate these shifts. If you find yourself at a crossroads, take time for introspection, and open your intuitive channels for divine guidance. Trust that your Pleiadian ancestry will endow you with the wisdom and courage to walk the path that serves your highest good.

Summary

Your career and life purpose are not isolated elements of your Earthly experience but are intertwined with your larger cosmic mission. By adopting a Pleiadian perspective on vocation, you transition from a rigid, Earth-centric viewpoint to one that encompasses a galactic sense of purpose. When you align your career choices with your soul contract, you not only find fulfillment but also contribute positively to both Earth and the greater cosmos. And through it all, remain adaptable and open to change, for the universe is dynamic, and so is the grand purpose it has for you.

CHAPTER 4: PLEIADIAN PRACTICES FOR EMOTIONAL WELL-BEING

Introduction

Emotional well-being is a core aspect of living a fulfilling life, both on Earth and in the Pleiades. It is especially vital for Pleiadian Starseeds, who are often more sensitive to emotional energies. This heightened sensitivity can be a blessing but may also present its challenges. This chapter explores some time-tested Pleiadian practices aimed at enhancing emotional well-being, allowing you to harmonize your energies and cultivate a sense of inner peace.

Emotional Landscaping: Visualization Techniques

One of the most potent tools in the Pleiadian emotional wellness toolkit is visualization, specifically emotional landscaping. This involves envisioning your emotional state as a vivid landscape. It can be anything—a serene beach, a bustling city, a tranquil forest, or even an abstract realm. This landscape serves as a metaphor for your emotional world, making abstract feelings more tangible.

In this practice, you close your eyes and immerse yourself in this landscape, taking note of each detail. For instance, if you find a stormy ocean, it could symbolize turbulent emotions. You can then imagine calming the ocean's waves, which acts as a metaphorical means of soothing your emotional unrest. The idea is that by altering the landscape in your visualization, you can influence your emotional state in the physical world. With regular practice, you'll find that your emotional self gains a degree of resilience and flexibility.

Energetic Hygiene: Clearing Emotional Blockages

Energetic hygiene focuses on maintaining the cleanliness and flow of your energy system, which is closely tied to your emotional well-being. In Pleiadian tradition, it is believed that emotions are not just psychological but also energetic phenomena. Therefore, negative emotions or traumas can cause blockages in your energetic flow. These blockages can manifest as emotional turmoil, physical ailments, or even chronic fatigue.

To practice energetic hygiene, first, become aware of your emotional state. Scan your body for areas of tension or discomfort, often indicators of blocked energy. The next step is to focus on your breath. Visualize breathing in positive energy and breathing out negative energy. The idea is to dissolve or at least soften these blockages.

Some Pleiadians also use sound healing for this purpose. Tuning forks or singing bowls that produce specific frequencies can align with your body's energy centers, or chakras, to facilitate flow and release. Though sound healing instruments may not be readily available, even humming a tone that resonates with you can be beneficial.

The Akashic Dialogue: Accessing Higher Wisdom

The Akashic Records are believed to be a cosmic repository containing the knowledge of every soul's experience. Pleiadians often consult these records for insights into emotional patterns or issues. Unlike conventional therapy, which focuses on the linear timeline of one's life, the Akashic Dialogue allows for a more expansive perspective that spans multiple lifetimes and even parallel realities.

To access the Akashic Records, you'll need to enter a meditative state and seek permission from your higher self or spiritual guides. Once granted, ask specific questions related to your emotional challenges. The answers often come as intuitive impressions, images, or feelings rather than direct verbal responses. These insights can help you understand the root causes of your emotional disturbances and offer solutions for achieving balance.

Summary

Emotional well-being is not merely a state but an ongoing practice, requiring awareness, active engagement, and periodic introspection. The Pleiadian approaches discussed in this chapter—emotional landscaping for self-awareness, energetic hygiene for clearing blockages, and Akashic Dialogue for higher wisdom—offer an integrative roadmap to emotional wellness. By adopting these practices, you can navigate the ups and downs of earthly life more effectively, harmonize your energies, and fulfill your role as a Pleiadian Starseed with greater resilience and joy.

CHAPTER 5: NAVIGATING EARTHLY SYSTEMS: POLITICS, ECONOMICS, AND SOCIAL STRUCTURES

In an increasingly interconnected world, the intricacies of Earth's systems can often feel overwhelming. For Pleiadian Starseeds who may be inherently attuned to higher frequencies of unity and cooperation, these earthly frameworks can sometimes seem complicated, if not outright perplexing. This chapter aims to shed light on how Pleiadian wisdom can inform and guide us through the complex mazes of politics, economics, and social systems, helping us navigate these structures with enhanced clarity, fairness, and effectiveness.

The Pleiadian Perspective on Politics

Pleiadians, as members of the Galactic Federation, have governance structures that focus on unity, transparency, and collective well-being. The divisive and often polarized nature of Earth's political systems might make it challenging for Starseeds to engage effectively. Nevertheless, Pleiadian wisdom encourages active involvement, recognizing that constructive change can only come through participation.

One key Pleiadian concept is the principle of co-creative governance, where every individual's voice is honored and used to build consensus. Applying this principle to Earth's political systems suggests a more participatory approach. Consider becoming more involved in local governance, advocating for transparent decision-making, and pushing for electoral systems that allow for proportional representation. Even if these principles seem lofty or utopian by Earth's current standards, their gradual introduction can serve as a beacon for systemic transformation.

Pleiadian Economic Philosophy

The economic systems on Pleiades operate on a foundation of abundance and equitable distribution of resources. This is in stark contrast to Earth's prevailing economic systems, which often focus on competition and accumulation. For Pleiadian Starseeds, the disparity between these paradigms can create a sense of dissonance.

However, it's crucial to remember that you can act as catalysts for change. The Pleiadian understanding of abundance is rooted in the belief that the Universe is inherently generous. Adopting this perspective allows for a broader view of economics, extending beyond just monetary wealth. The focus shifts towards sustainability, environmental stewardship, and community well-being. On a practical level, this could manifest as supporting sustainable business models, advocating for equitable wealth distribution, and challenging materialism as a measure of success. Initiatives like community gardens, local currencies, and cooperatives are good starting points for embodying Pleiadian economic philosophies.

Pleiadian Principles in Social Structures

Pleiadian society places a premium on interconnectedness, understanding that each individual's actions reverberate throughout the collective. Earth's current social systems often compartmentalize aspects of human life into silos like education, healthcare, and criminal justice, losing sight of the interconnected nature of these sectors.

To bring Pleiadian wisdom into these structures, Starseeds might focus on holistic solutions. For example, educational systems could benefit from a more rounded curriculum that includes emotional intelligence, ecological awareness, and intercultural understanding, alongside traditional academic subjects. In the realm of healthcare, holistic approaches could integrate mental and emotional well-being into the larger picture of physical health. By weaving the Pleiadian principles of interconnectedness, compassion, and collective well-being into the fabric of these institutions, meaningful transformation can be enacted.

Summary

Navigating Earth's complex systems of politics, economics, and social structures is a daunting task, especially for Pleiadian Starseeds, who may find these systems antithetical to their intrinsic values. However, the Pleiadian perspective offers valuable insights for reimagining and reforming these structures from within. Whether it's advocating for a more participatory form of governance, pushing for economic systems rooted in abundance and fairness, or integrating a more interconnected approach into social services, the Pleiadian wisdom offers practical and transformative solutions. By applying these principles, Starseeds not only make these systems more bearable for themselves but also pave the way for a more harmonious Earth, aligned with galactic virtues of unity and collective well-being.

PART XI: ETHICS AND RESPONSIBILITIES

CHAPTER 1: FREE WILL AND PREDESTINATION

Introduction

The question of free will versus predestination has been a subject of philosophical inquiry for millennia. Within the context of Pleiadian philosophy and ethics, this matter takes on added layers of complexity. Given their advanced understanding of time, space, and the interconnectedness of all things, Pleiadians offer unique perspectives on these concepts. This chapter aims to shed light on how Pleiadians view the dynamic interplay between free will and predestination, and what implications this has for your role as a Starseed in the larger cosmic scheme.

The Pleiadian Perspective on Free Will

Free will, in the Pleiadian worldview, is the divine gift that allows a soul to make choices that align with its unique purpose and developmental needs. Free will is considered a fundamental aspect of sentient existence. Pleiadians believe that every being is a co-creator in this vast, intricate web of existence. In exercising free will, you participate in the creative processes that bring events and experiences into manifestation. The intention behind a choice can serve as a catalyst for growth and transformation, not only for the individual making the choice but also for the collective consciousness.

This concept of free will aligns closely with the Pleiadian understanding of "Creative Choice," which is a concept that elevates the mere act of choosing to a spiritually generative force. Creative Choice recognizes that your choices have repercussions in multiple dimensions and timelines, influencing not only your own soul journey but also those of other beings interconnected with your life. Therefore, exercising free will comes with an ethical responsibility to choose wisely, keeping in mind the broader consequences of one's actions.

The Pleiadian Conception of Predestination

On the flip side, Pleiadians also acknowledge the role of predestination, particularly through the lens of Soul Contracts and the Akashic Records. Before incarnating into a physical form, souls make agreements or contracts outlining specific experiences, relationships, and challenges they wish to encounter. This blueprint serves as a guiding structure for the soul's journey. Yet, it is not fixed or immutable; rather, it can be revised based on the choices made and the lessons learned.

Predestination, in this sense, serves as a sort of cosmic map or GPS system. While there are predetermined "waypoints" on your journey, how you reach these points and what you learn along the way remains an open question, subject to the exercise of free will. Thus, predestination doesn't negate free will but rather works in tandem with it, providing a balance between structure and spontaneity.

Harmonizing Free Will and Predestination

Pleiadian philosophy posits that free will and predestination are not mutually exclusive; instead, they exist in a dynamic equilibrium. Imagine a dance where one partner leads while the other follows, yet both contribute to the beauty and grace of the performance. In a similar fashion, free will and predestination interact in a delicate balance to create the unique tapestry of your life experience.

This harmonizing perspective is vital for Starseeds who may find themselves torn between their earthly desires and their cosmic obligations. Understanding that you have both the liberty to choose and a predetermined purpose can help you navigate life with greater wisdom and ethical clarity. Your choices become mindful acts of co-creation with the Universe, guided by the higher wisdom encoded in your soul contract.

Summary

The Pleiadian perspective on free will and predestination offers a balanced view that honors both individual agency and the overarching cosmic plan. By seeing these concepts as complementary rather than contradictory, Pleiadians approach life with a sense of purposeful freedom. For Starseeds, understanding this balance can bring about a richer, more nuanced view of existence, facilitating a deeper alignment with both earthly and galactic responsibilities. Whether you're making a simple choice or a life-altering decision, the Pleiadian wisdom teaches that your free will operates within a framework of cosmic order, offering both freedom and direction in your soul's journey.

CHAPTER 2: PLEIADIAN ETHICS ON HEALING AND MANIPULATING ENERGIES

Introduction

The concept of energy manipulation and healing has long been a cornerstone in Pleiadian spiritual practice and understanding. However, the ethical implications that come with such abilities are of equal importance. This chapter delves into the ethics that Pleiadians hold regarding the manipulation and healing of energies, both for self and others, to ensure that these practices are aligned with the higher moral and spiritual principles of the Galactic Family.

Ethical Boundaries in Energy Healing

Energy healing is one of the most profound gifts that Pleiadians possess and can bestow. From subtle calibrations of emotional energies to the more intricate and complex balancing of spiritual frequencies, energy healing serves as a tool for harmonization and wellbeing. But like all forms of power, it comes with responsibilities. Pleiadians believe that the ethical framework around energy healing starts with "Informed Consent." This means that no healing should ever occur without the express agreement of the one being healed. Whether on a physical, emotional, or spiritual level, each individual has their sovereign right to their own energy space, and breaching that without permission is considered one of the highest ethical violations.

Moreover, Pleiadians maintain the doctrine of "First, Do No Harm." Healers must ensure that they themselves are in a balanced and ethical state before engaging in healing practices. One cannot pour from an empty cup, and a misaligned healer could inadvertently transfer their imbalances to the one they are healing. Precautions, such as self-purification rituals and emotional grounding exercises, are usually undertaken before engaging in any healing acts.

The Ethics of Energy Manipulation

Aside from healing, the ability to manipulate energies extends to a broader spectrum that may include telepathic influence, emotional resonance, and even altering physical circumstances around them. While these abilities can serve powerful functions for protection, growth, and communal harmony, they can easily be misused.

Pleiadians abide by the principle of "Respect for Free Will" when it comes to energy manipulation. Any act that seeks to control, rather than guide or assist, is considered an infringement of another being's free will. For example, manipulating someone's emotions to make them feel a certain way towards you is an unethical use of this ability. There's a clear difference between supporting someone's emotional state and trying to change it to fit your own needs or desires.

In essence, the ethical boundary here is set by the intent behind the manipulation. Is the act motivated by a selfless desire to assist another, or is it rooted in self-interest, control, or manipulation? The discernment of intent is vital in evaluating the ethical nature of any act involving energy manipulation.

Universal Consequences

Pleiadians strongly believe in the interconnectedness of all things. An act of energy manipulation or healing is not isolated but sends ripples across the energetic universe. Ethical lapses in this area can have far-reaching consequences that may not be immediately visible. Thus, they follow the concept of "Karmic Responsibility," where each action taken—positive or negative—will eventually come back to the individual in some form, reinforcing the importance of acting ethically and responsibly.

Summary

Pleiadian ethics concerning healing and energy manipulation are grounded in the principles of informed consent, do no harm, respect for free will, and karmic responsibility. The ethical guidelines act as a framework to ensure that these powerful abilities are used judiciously, respectfully, and for the greater good. An understanding of these ethics is crucial for any Pleiadian Starseed as they navigate their abilities and roles within the broader Galactic Family, maintaining a harmonious balance within themselves and the energies they interact with.

CHAPTER 3: THE UNIVERSAL LAW OF ONE

The concept of "The Universal Law of One" holds a special place in Pleiadian ethics and serves as the bedrock for understanding the interconnectedness of all beings, whether terrestrial or extraterrestrial. Essentially, this law encapsulates the belief in the fundamental unity of all life forms, not just within a single planet or solar system, but across the Universe. To gain a fuller comprehension of this deeply ingrained Pleiadian belief, let's delve into the various facets of the Universal Law of One, its implications for ethics and behavior, and how it is practiced by Pleiadian starseeds on Earth.

Essence of the Universal Law of One

The Universal Law of One postulates that all is One and One is all. In this understanding, individual consciousness is merely a part of a larger, cosmic consciousness. The law suggests that every action, thought, or emotion influences this cosmic web, thereby affecting every other entity within it. This is not an abstract concept for Pleiadians; rather, it is a lived reality. From the energy they harness for technologies to the way they interact with other civilizations, the Law of One is integrated into every aspect of Pleiadian life.

Ethical Implications

Given that the Law of One propounds that all actions ripple through the collective consciousness, it bears immense ethical implications. For Pleiadians, actions are not evaluated solely based on their immediate or localized impact but are gauged against a universal moral fabric. This is especially critical when engaging in activities like energy manipulation, as discussed in the previous chapter, where the actions have the potential to affect the life-forces of multiple entities.

Acting in ways that harmonize with the Law of One also diminishes karmic debt, a concept familiar to Pleiadians. While they believe that certain life circumstances are predestined, as covered in earlier chapters, the Law of One teaches that ethical conduct reduces the negative karmic residues that an individual carries, thus facilitating spiritual ascension and inner peace.

The Law of One in Practice: Pleiadian Starseeds on Earth

For Pleiadian starseeds living on Earth, adhering to the Universal Law of One often comes as an intuitive, natural inclination. However, the dense energies and conflicting belief systems on Earth can sometimes make it challenging to consistently practice this law. Pleiadian starseeds may find themselves torn between the earthly ways of individualism and competition and their innate pull toward unity and collective well-being.

Nonetheless, there are several ways starseeds can enact the Law of One in their earthly lives:

1. Through acts of compassion and kindness, not just toward fellow humans but all forms of life, recognizing the divine spark within each.

2. By engaging in professions or activities that serve the greater good. Many Pleiadian starseeds are naturally drawn to fields like healthcare, environmental conservation, and social justice.

3. By cultivating inner harmony through spiritual practices like meditation, energy healing, or even simply spending time in nature, thereby raising their vibrational frequency, which positively affects the collective consciousness.

4. Through responsible consumption, be it of food, media, or energy, always keeping in mind the interconnected web of life.

In practicing the Universal Law of One, starseeds not only enhance their own spiritual evolution but contribute to Earth's collective ascension, harmonizing with their Pleiadian ethos of universal unity and responsibility.

Summary

The Universal Law of One is a cornerstone in Pleiadian philosophy, symbolizing the interconnected nature of all existence. This foundational belief informs the ethical and spiritual practices of Pleiadians, who view every action, thought, and emotion as an integral part of a cosmic whole. Pleiadian starseeds, even when on Earth, are guided by this principle, endeavoring to live in ways that honor and promote unity and collective well-being. Through understanding and practicing the Universal Law of One, starseeds align themselves more closely with their Pleiadian heritage and actively participate in the elevation of collective consciousness.

CHAPTER 4: THE GALACTIC FEDERATION: STRUCTURE AND GOVERNANCE

Introduction

The topic of the Galactic Federation is one that deeply intrigues many Starseeds and spiritually minded individuals. As Pleiadian Starseeds, understanding the Galactic Federation's structure and governance can provide valuable insight into the broader cosmic picture, your role within it, and how the Pleiades fit into this intricate framework. This chapter will delve into the hierarchical structure, key responsibilities, and the ethical guidelines followed by this interstellar alliance.

Hierarchical Structure

The Galactic Federation is often visualized as a pyramid of collaborative entities and civilizations, each contributing according to their capacities and specialized knowledge. At the apex of the pyramid sits a council of highly evolved beings, known colloquially as the "High Council." They are responsible for making critical decisions affecting the Federation and its members, including Pleiadians.

Below the High Council are various subsidiary councils, specialized in areas like science, spirituality, and diplomacy, among others. Each star system, including the Pleiadian star system, has its own local council that acts as an intermediary between the planetary governments and the Federation's higher tiers. The Pleiadian Council, for example, represents Pleiadian interests and brings forth the collective wisdom and contributions of the Pleiades to the Federation.

Key Responsibilities and Functions

The Galactic Federation serves several primary functions designed to maintain peace, facilitate evolution, and uphold cosmic law. One of its main roles is mediating conflicts between different civilizations and worlds. This peacekeeping mission is of great importance, especially when planetary civilizations go through significant transitions, as it helps to avert cosmic chaos.

Another crucial function is the sharing and regulation of advanced technologies, especially those with the potential for misuse. Many of these technologies are beyond human comprehension, dealing with matters such as time manipulation, cosmic energy harnessing, and dimensional travel. By regulating technology dissemination, the Federation ensures that advanced capabilities don't fall into the wrong hands, either by mistake or design.

Additionally, the Federation plays a role in guiding spiritual evolution. It assists planetary civilizations, including Earth, in their ascension processes by sharing spiritual teachings, advanced healing techniques, and by raising the vibrational frequencies of these worlds subtly. This is often achieved through emissaries or Starseeds, who incarnate on these planets to act as way-showers. The Federation's collective wisdom in spirituality is an amalgamation of the knowledge and spiritual practices of all its member civilizations, which include the Pleiadians.

Ethical Guidelines

The Galactic Federation operates on a robust ethical framework. One cornerstone is the Law of Free Will, which stipulates that no civilization can impose its will, beliefs, or technologies upon another without explicit consent. This is where the Pleiadian understanding of ethics, discussed in previous chapters, converges with the Federation's principles.

Another crucial ethical tenet is the principle of Non-Interference. Member civilizations, including the Pleiadians, must adhere to this guideline, particularly when dealing with planets like Earth that are still in the early stages of spiritual evolution. Exceptions are made in extreme circumstances, but these are rare and require collective approval from the High Council.

The Federation also places great emphasis on the Universal Law of One, recognizing the interconnectedness of all life forms and civilizations. This shared understanding encourages cooperation, mutual respect, and a sense of collective responsibility towards the evolution of the universe.

Summary

Understanding the Galactic Federation's structure, responsibilities, and ethical guidelines offers Pleiadian Starseeds a broader perspective on their cosmic journey. The Federation acts as a mediator, a regulator, and a spiritual guide for its members. Its existence exemplifies unity in diversity, bringing together various civilizations, including the Pleiadians, under a shared set of ethical and spiritual principles. As you continue to explore your Pleiadian heritage and mission on Earth, this understanding can serve as a compass, aligning you more closely with the objectives of the Galactic Federation and, by extension, your role in this cosmic symphony.

CHAPTER 5: STARSEED ETHICS IN HUMAN SOCIETY

Introduction

The journey of a Pleiadian Starseed is profoundly intricate, threaded through both earthly and galactic dimensions. As you've delved into Pleiadian ethics, cosmology, and spiritual practices, you're likely brimming with new perceptions and an enriched understanding of your cosmic origins. Yet, this newfound wisdom begs a crucial question: How does one apply these universal ethics to life on Earth? This chapter aims to provide an in-depth exploration of the Starseed's ethical responsibilities within human society, examining the harmonious convergence of Pleiadian principles with earthly existence.

Transcultural Respect

One of the foremost responsibilities for Pleiadian Starseeds is the promotion and embodiment of transcultural respect. As beings who have memories or intuitions of lives in different star systems, you hold a broader view of cultures and civilizations. Yet, Earth has its own multi-layered tapestry of cultures, each with its unique set of values, traditions, and ethical frameworks.

Balancing your galactic identity with respect for earthly cultures can be intricate but is necessary.

Remember, the core Pleiadian ethics, such as the Universal Law of One, focus on unity and interconnectedness. As such, acknowledging the richness of Earth's cultural diversity while recognizing the universal threads that connect all forms of life is essential. But respect goes beyond mere acknowledgment; it involves active listening, open dialogue, and a willingness to understand perspectives that may seem foreign to your galactic sensibilities. It's about engaging with humanity without superimposing your star-born beliefs in a way that dismisses or devalues Earth's own rich traditions and philosophies.

Ethical Interventions in Earthly Affairs

Given your heightened sensitivities, unique gifts, and a broader understanding of energies, you may often feel the urge to intervene in human affairs. While this is laudable, it's crucial to exercise discernment. Pleiadian ethics don't give carte blanche to manipulate energies or circumstances solely because you perceive a greater good from your vantage point.

The concept of Free Will, as discussed in earlier chapters, is sacrosanct not just in galactic dimensions but also on Earth. Ethical interventions should ideally be consent-based and carried out with profound respect for all parties involved. Whether you are using Pleiadian healing modalities, energy work, or even sharing wisdom, the free will of others is a boundary that must be honored.

Remember, not everyone on Earth is at the same point in their spiritual journey. The most ethical way to offer intervention is to be available, providing guidance when asked, and refraining from imposing your galactic insights or spiritual techniques upon others without explicit permission. This aligns well with the Pleiadian ethical framework that respects individual sovereignty while promoting collective wellbeing.

Ethical Stewardship of Earth

Lastly, your ethical responsibilities also extend to Earth as a living being. The Pleiadian approach to sustainable living, as discussed in previous chapters, provides a blueprint for ecological responsibility. Taking steps to reduce your carbon footprint, advocating for the protection of natural resources, and educating others about the importance of environmental stewardship are aligned with both Pleiadian ethics and urgent earthly needs.

In this sense, your role as a Pleiadian Starseed places you in a unique position to act as a bridge between celestial wisdom and earthly practicalities. Ethical stewardship means not just advocating for a better world, but actively participating in its creation through daily choices, advocacy, and education.

Summary

Navigating the ethical landscape as a Pleiadian Starseed within human society involves a dynamic interplay of celestial wisdom and earthly practicalities. The key lies in nurturing transcultural respect, exercising ethical discernment when intervening in human affairs, and embracing the stewardship of Earth as a living entity. By integrating these principles into your daily life, you continue to honor your Pleiadian lineage while fulfilling your earthly mission. In doing so, you become a living example of how the wisdom of the stars can illuminate the complexities of human existence, fostering a more harmonious, interconnected world.

PART XII: UPCOMING GALACTIC EVENTS

CHAPTER 1: THE GREAT AWAKENING: WHAT TO EXPECT

Introduction

As we navigate through this grand voyage of understanding your Pleiadian Starseed origins, your role in the Galactic Family, and the multidimensional aspects of your being, it's critical to turn our attention to the horizon of upcoming galactic events. Foremost among these is what many term "The Great Awakening." In this chapter, we will delve into what this concept means, what you can anticipate, and how it aligns with Pleiadian teachings and outlooks.

The Concept of The Great Awakening

The Great Awakening is a term used to describe a colossal shift in collective consciousness. It's a period marked by the rapid acceleration of spiritual understanding, psychic abilities, and a unified sense of purpose that transcends traditional boundaries of nationality, religion, and culture. For Pleiadian Starseeds and other cosmic wanderers, this time represents a juncture where your skills, wisdom, and insights will be most needed.

In the Pleiadian view, The Great Awakening isn't an isolated Earthly event but part of a larger galactic momentum. Think of it as a synchronicity on a cosmic scale, where multiple timelines, dimensions, and sentient races find a point of convergence. During this phase, the Veil that separates the physical from the spiritual, the known from the unknown, becomes permeable, allowing for an easier exchange of energies and information between dimensions.

The Role of Starseeds and Lightworkers

As a Pleiadian Starseed, you are not a passive spectator in this awakening. You are, in many ways, a catalyst. Your vibrational frequency, elevated understanding of unity consciousness, and inherent empathic abilities are tools that can aid in the collective transformation. While the journey will be deeply personal, involving intense periods of self-examination and soul evolution, it also has an undeniable social aspect. You'll find yourself drawn to acts that serve the greater good, often in innovative and inspiring ways.

The Great Awakening also aligns closely with the Pleiadian concept of "The Quickening," a term used in Pleiades to describe a universal uptick in vibrational frequency. For many Starseeds, this will be a time where dormant DNA activations may occur, granting access to latent psychic gifts like telepathy, clairvoyance, or energy manipulation. Therefore, staying grounded while also open to these emerging abilities will be crucial.

Signs, Milestones, and Practical Preparation

The progression towards The Great Awakening is not linear and will manifest differently for each individual. However, there are some signs and milestones to be aware of:

1. **Increased Synchronicities:** Sequences of numbers, meeting people who feel like "soul family," and unexplainable coincidences can serve as guideposts that you are on the right path.

2. **Heightened Intuition:** A sharper sense of gut feeling or sudden insights that seem to come 'out of the blue' are often indicators of your expanding consciousness.

3. **Collective Challenges:** Periods of societal upheaval, including political instability or environmental crises, often precede large-scale awakenings. These challenges serve as catalysts that break down old systems to make way for new paradigms.

4. **Inner Transformation:** Emotional releases, revisiting old wounds to heal them, and profound dreams are signs that your internal world is preparing for a significant shift.

Preparing for these eventualities involves a mix of mental, physical, and spiritual readiness. Regular meditation, keeping a dream journal, maintaining a balanced lifestyle, and staying connected with your Pleiadian guides and soul family are useful practices. Strengthening your grounding techniques will also be critical as the energies intensify.

Summary

The Great Awakening is a significant event that promises to usher in a new era of collective consciousness, both on Earth and across the galaxy. As a Pleiadian Starseed, you play an integral role in this cosmic shift. Your inherent abilities not only serve your personal growth but are also invaluable tools that can help humanity navigate this transformative period. By understanding the signs and knowing how to prepare, you equip yourself to be a beacon of light, guiding others as we all move toward a more enlightened state of being.

CHAPTER 2: THE ASCENSION PROCESS: HOW IT AFFECTS YOU

Introduction

You've reached a crucial chapter in your journey of understanding your Pleiadian lineage and the part you play in the larger cosmic narrative. Here, we delve into the transformative experience commonly known as the "Ascension Process." This is an event many Starseeds, not just Pleiadian, believe they are destined to partake in, a monumental elevation of consciousness that affects not only individual souls but also the collective. Let's explore what this entails, the stages involved, and most importantly, how it directly impacts you.

The Core Essence of Ascension

Ascension, in a metaphysical context, refers to the process of elevating one's vibrational frequency to align more closely with higher-dimensional states of consciousness. This is not merely a shift in perception; it's a biological, psychological, and spiritual metamorphosis. While there are multiple theories and approaches to understanding ascension, Pleiadians have a unique view rooted in their history and cosmic ethos. They see this process as integral to the evolution of any civilization, but particularly pressing for Earth at this pivotal time in its history. In Pleiadian philosophy, ascension is not an event but a continuous process. It's akin to a spiraling ladder where you may revisit certain themes or lessons but from a higher vantage point. It involves shedding old energies, paradigms, and limitations, and embracing a new state of existence where unity, compassion, and higher wisdom are not lofty ideals but lived realities.

How Ascension Affects Your Physical and Energetic Bodies

The impact of the ascension process is profound and multidimensional. Let's consider first its influence on your physical and energetic bodies:

Physical Body:

The biological vessel you inhabit is not just a mass of cells but a complex system sensitive to energetic shifts. During ascension, it's common to experience a range of physical symptoms, such as unusual fatigue, heightened sensitivity to foods and substances, or even mysterious aches and pains. These are often signs of the body readjusting to higher frequencies.

Energetic Body:

Your aura or energetic field undergoes a significant transformation as well. Old energy patterns and blockages start to dissolve, making way for new formations of light and energy that better serve your higher self. This may also manifest as heightened intuitive abilities, such as clairvoyance, telepathy, or a deepened sense of empathy.

The Stages of Ascension: A Pleiadian Perspective

From the Pleiadian point of view, ascension unfolds through distinct stages, each serving a specific purpose in your spiritual advancement. Here they are in a condensed format:

1. **Awakening**: The initial realization that there is more to reality than the material world. It's when you begin questioning longstanding beliefs and become aware of your spiritual lineage.
2. **Purification**: This involves the cleansing of old energies, beliefs, and karmic patterns that no longer serve you. It's a challenging but necessary phase.
3. **Integration**: Here, you start to integrate higher frequencies and wisdom into your daily life. New spiritual practices may be adopted, and you begin to live from a place of greater authenticity.
4. **Embodiment**: In this stage, you become a living representation of the higher dimensions on Earth. Your very presence becomes a catalyst for change and transformation for those around you.

Summary

The ascension process, from the Pleiadian perspective, is an intricate, multi-layered journey that is both deeply personal and collectively significant. It affects all aspects of your being, from your physical body to your energetic makeup, forcing you to confront old paradigms and embrace new states of consciousness. The Pleiadians see this not as an end but as an essential chapter in an ongoing, spiraled narrative of soul evolution. Understanding the stages of ascension can provide a roadmap, helping you to navigate this transformative experience with a sense of purpose and clarity. While challenges are an integral part of this journey, they are but stepping stones on your path to becoming a more enlightened, multidimensional version of yourself.

CHAPTER 3: COSMIC CYCLES AND THEIR INFLUENCE

Introduction

In this chapter, we will delve into an essential aspect of understanding your role in the galactic family: cosmic cycles. These are recurring events or phenomena that occur at both macrocosmic and microcosmic levels, influencing all forms of life in the universe. For Pleiadian Starseeds, comprehending these cycles offers a nuanced perspective on the interconnectedness of cosmic phenomena and individual life paths.

The Concept of Cosmic Cycles

The idea of cosmic cycles is foundational to Pleiadian cosmology, resonating with the ancient wisdom of earthly traditions like the Mayan and Vedic calendars. In Pleiadian thought, the universe doesn't move in a straight line but in a circle. Cycles govern everything from the revolution of planets to the evolution of galaxies and the progression of souls. These cycles are not merely time-bound events but are imprinted with energies that influence the collective and individual consciousness.

There are many types of cosmic cycles, but a few stand out for their significance. The Great Year, also known as the Precession of the Equinoxes, is one such cycle, lasting about 25,920 Earth years. It's during this period that the Earth makes one complete cycle through the twelve zodiacal constellations. According to Pleiadian wisdom, each Great Year heralds significant shifts in consciousness and triggers activations in Starseeds and other galactic beings. Understanding where we currently stand in this Great Year can offer insights into the nature of unfolding events, both globally and personally.

The Impact on Pleiadian Starseeds

Pleiadian Starseeds are deeply influenced by these cosmic cycles, perhaps more so than other types of Starseeds. The reason is that Pleiadian souls are intrinsically attuned to the harmonics of these cosmic rhythms. As cycles reach their peak or transition phases, many Starseeds report experiencing heightened intuition, vivid dreams, or even physical symptoms like sudden fatigue or bursts of energy. These are not random occurrences but are indicative of a greater synchronicity at play, aligning individual experiences with cosmic events.

For example, the culmination of smaller cycles within the Great Year can result in specific "activation windows" for Pleiadian Starseeds. During these periods, you may find that your psychic abilities amplify or that you receive more direct guidance from your Pleiadian guides. Moreover, these cycles often correspond with earthly events such as solar flares, lunar cycles, and planetary alignments, making their influence doubly potent.

One more nuanced aspect is the influence of cosmic cycles on your life mission. Understanding your role within these cycles can offer valuable insights into your earthly objectives and galactic responsibilities. It may reveal why you chose to incarnate during this particular period and what lessons or contributions you are meant to focus on.

Practical Applications: Aligning with Cosmic Cycles

Aligning with these cycles is not just a matter of esoteric curiosity; it has practical applications in your life. Here are some ways to synchronize with these cosmic rhythms:

1. **Astrological Study**: Keeping track of significant planetary alignments and zodiac transitions can provide cues for personal growth and understanding your mission better.
2. **Meditation and Introspection**: Utilize periods of cosmic significance for deep meditation and introspection. Ask for guidance or clarity regarding your path and responsibilities.
3. **Community Gatherings**: As these cycles impact the collective, engaging in community activities or ceremonies during key phases can amplify their positive effects.

By tuning into these cycles consciously, you become more than a passive spectator; you become an active participant in the unfolding of the cosmos, fulfilling your role in the galactic family.

Summary

Cosmic cycles serve as the hidden choreographers of universal events and individual experiences. They offer a structure that helps Pleiadian Starseeds and other cosmic entities understand their place in the grand cosmic design. While their influence is complex and multi-layered, aligning with these cycles can provide profound insights into your earthly mission and spiritual growth. As you become aware of these cosmic rhythms, you not only enrich your own journey but also contribute to the collective ascension process that impacts all beings across galaxies.

CHAPTER 4: EARTH CHANGES: PLEIADIAN PERSPECTIVES

Introduction

As we journey through the multifaceted realm of Pleiadian wisdom and understanding, one cannot overlook the imminent changes Earth is undergoing—changes that not only affect humanity but have reverberations across the galaxy. This chapter aims to offer the Pleiadian perspectives on these changes, encompassing everything from climate shifts to tectonic activity, and how these alterations align with cosmic cycles and energies.

Earth Changes in the Context of Cosmic Cycles

Earth is not a standalone entity; it is deeply intertwined with the cosmic web of existence. According to Pleiadian beliefs, the planet's evolutionary trajectory is synchronized with larger cosmic cycles, such as the Great Year, which is a period of approximately 26,000 Earth years. This cycle is said to influence the Earth's position relative to the galactic core, affecting everything from Earth's magnetic fields to climate and consciousness.

Pleiadians contend that as we near the zenith of this cycle, Earth undergoes a series of transformative changes. This could mean increased tectonic activity like earthquakes, volcanic eruptions, and changes in ocean currents. While from a human perspective these might seem like catastrophic events, Pleiadians view them as necessary recalibrations aimed at energetic realignment. The physical changes mirror the energetic shifts occurring on a cosmic scale, preparing Earth and its inhabitants for a higher state of being.

The Pleiadian Outlook on Earth's Ecological Shifts

Environmental degradation, climate change, and loss of biodiversity are critical issues from a Pleiadian standpoint as well. The Pleiadians often express a certain degree of concern and compassion about the rapid changes induced by human activity, which they see as out of sync with the Earth's natural rhythms. They encourage humanity to adopt a more sustainable approach that aligns with the planet's energetic balance. From the Pleiadian perspective, current ecological crises are not just human-made but are signs of Earth's struggle to adjust to new cosmic energies. They believe that adopting more harmonious living practices could help ease this transitional phase, reducing the severity of natural disasters and imbalances.

The Pleiadian philosophy holds that Earth is a sentient being, Gaia, who is undergoing her own evolutionary journey. Human actions that contribute to ecological imbalance are considered not only harmful to Earth but also to the cosmic equilibrium. The Pleiadians emphasize the importance of collective consciousness in healing the planet. Simple acts like tree planting, soil conservation, and adopting renewable energy sources are considered to be in energetic alignment with Gaia's needs.

Implications for Starseeds and Humanity

Understanding Earth changes from a Pleiadian viewpoint can offer Starseeds a deeper sense of purpose and belonging. As Earth navigates through these critical junctures, the role of Starseeds becomes ever more significant. They serve as conduits of higher-dimensional energies, helping to harmonize the disruptive changes taking place. It's a symbiotic relationship: just as the Earth offers Starseeds a platform for their spiritual evolution, they can reciprocate by assisting Earth in its own transformation.

The Pleiadians suggest that Starseeds engage in Earth-healing activities, whether it's by working directly with environmental causes or by incorporating Earth-friendly practices into their daily lives. Furthermore, Starseeds can utilize their advanced empathic, telepathic, and intuitive abilities to sense the needs of the planet and respond accordingly. By tuning into Earth's energetic grids, they can help channel cosmic energies in ways that are beneficial for the planet's transition to a higher state of consciousness.

Summary

The Pleiadian perspective on Earth changes offers an expansive viewpoint that interlinks the planet's physical transformations with cosmic cycles and energies. Pleiadians consider Earth to be an evolving entity whose journey is synchronized with larger cosmic rhythms. They believe that current Earth changes are not merely catastrophes but are part of a larger recalibration process, influenced by cosmic energies. From this viewpoint, Starseeds, particularly those of Pleiadian origin, have a crucial role to play in facilitating this cosmic alignment. By understanding these dynamics, Starseeds can contribute positively to Earth's evolution, thereby fulfilling an integral part of their galactic mission.

CHAPTER 5: PREPARING FOR CONTACT: PRACTICAL STEPS

Introduction

As we near a pivotal period of human history, often referred to as "The Great Awakening" or "The Ascension," contact with higher-dimensional beings, including Pleiadians, becomes increasingly probable. This chapter offers a well-rounded guide to prepare emotionally, mentally, and spiritually for such an awe-inspiring event. Here, we'll look at some practical steps for readjusting your consciousness, setting intentions, and fostering the right environmental conditions for contact.

Elevating Consciousness and Emotional Preparedness

One of the first steps to make contact with Pleiadian energies or even physical entities is to elevate your consciousness to a frequency that aligns with theirs. This involves a deep self-assessment and cleansing of emotional blockages. Release fear-based emotions and thoughts, as fear serves as a frequency inhibitor, creating an energetic blockade between you and higher-dimensional entities.

Meditation is a powerful tool for this. Through meditation, you can access your subconscious mind, dispelling illusions and healing emotional scars. It helps in aligning your vibrational frequency with the Pleiadian energy matrix, thus facilitating easier contact. While some prefer silent, mindfulness-based meditations, others opt for guided journeys that lead them through a series of inner landscapes, aiding in this alignment. The choice is personal; what matters is that the method you choose is one that allows you to comfortably sink into a state of deep inner peace.

Setting Intentions and Creating Sacred Space

Your intentions hold immense power; they act like beacons, sending out a specific vibrational code into the Universe. Before trying to make contact, be clear about your intentions. Are you seeking guidance, companionship, or perhaps wisdom for personal or planetary healing? Whatever your reason, ensure it comes from a place of love and service, rather than curiosity or ego-based pursuits. Intentions rooted in service to the greater good resonate more closely with Pleiadian energies.

Setting up a sacred space can also serve as a catalyst for contact. This does not have to be elaborate but should be a place where you can sit quietly without being disturbed. You can include crystals known for facilitating cosmic contact like Moldavite, Selenite, or Clear Quartz, which we discussed in earlier chapters. Lighting a candle and playing soft, ambient music can further enhance the experience. This space serves as a physical manifestation of your intention and offers a harmonious setting where contact may take place.

Communication Protocols

While the idea of communicating with a higher-dimensional

being may seem intimidating, it's important to approach it like any other form of interaction—with respect and openness. Always ask for beings of the highest light and alignment with your highest good to come forward. This sets an energetic boundary for the contact experience.

Once contact is established, be it through a sensation, vision, or auditory message, express gratitude. Remember, communication can be more abstract than human language, taking the form of symbols, feelings, or instant "knowings." Keep a journal nearby to document your experiences. Writing down what you encounter can help you discern patterns and messages that may not be immediately obvious.

Summary

Preparing for contact with Pleiadian energies or beings is a multi-dimensional endeavor. It requires emotional and mental preparedness through elevating your consciousness and healing any emotional blockages. Setting the right intentions and creating a sacred space can not only send out the right vibrational signals but also offer a conducive environment for such profound interactions. Finally, when it comes to the actual contact, approach it with the same dignity and openness you would any meaningful interaction. The knowledge, companionship, and spiritual growth that could come from such contact are invaluable and can markedly accelerate your evolution as a Pleiadian Starseed and a member of the Galactic Family.

PART XIII: PLEIADIAN TOOLS AND TECHNOLOGIES

CHAPTER 1: ADVANCED PLEIADIAN HEALING INSTRUMENTS

Introduction

As we venture deeper into the expansive world of Pleiadian culture and wisdom, it's crucial to understand the technological advancements that set this star race apart. Pleiadians are not just spiritually advanced; they are also pioneers in employing avant-garde technologies, particularly in the field of healing. In this chapter, we delve into some of the groundbreaking Pleiadian healing instruments. Although you may not have direct access to these instruments, understanding their properties and functionalities can offer valuable insights into alternative healing modalities and how to integrate some of these principles into your life.

Crystalline Healing Pods

One of the most extraordinary Pleiadian inventions is the Crystalline Healing Pod. Constructed from a rare form of crystal only found in the Pleiades star cluster, this pod magnifies the natural healing energies of the universe. Users lie within the pod, and it is programmed to resonate with their unique energy signatures. The pod emits a harmonious symphony of light, sound, and vibration, custom-tailored to address specific ailments or imbalances in the physical or etheric bodies. The Crystalline Healing Pods are said to accelerate natural healing processes exponentially and can even tackle chronic or so-called "untreatable" conditions.

Frequency Harmonization Discs

Frequency Harmonization Discs are thin, plate-like objects inscribed with sacred geometry patterns. They function by aligning and harmonizing the vibrational frequencies of the environment or individual they are associated with. In healing contexts, these discs are placed under treatment tables or held in the hand during meditation or energy work. They are often programmed with specific intentions, much like how crystals are programmed on Earth, to amplify their healing potential. Utilizing these discs in conjunction with other forms of therapy can significantly increase the efficacy of the healing process.

Scalar Wave Projectors

Scalar Wave Projectors represent an apex in Pleiadian healing technologies. Scalar waves are capable of traveling faster than the speed of light and can penetrate any form of matter. They are neutral waves of energy and can carry information. In the Pleiadian healing context, Scalar Wave Projectors are used to transmit healing codes directly into the cellular and subatomic levels of the patient. This is particularly effective in the reprogramming of DNA and the eradication of harmful energetic patterns or imprints. This form of healing is usually administered by advanced healers trained in manipulating scalar energy and is not commonly used for self-healing.

Ethical Considerations

It's essential to note that while these technologies offer incredible healing capabilities, they are always employed in a manner that respects the individual's free will and soul contract. In Pleiadian ethics, healing is a cooperative process requiring consent and conscious participation from the person receiving the healing. The technology acts as an aid or a tool and is never considered a replacement for the innate healing capabilities of the individual.

Summary

The advanced healing technologies of the Pleiadian civilization open up avenues for understanding the intricate union of science and spirituality. These tools, such as Crystalline Healing Pods, Frequency Harmonization Discs, and Scalar Wave Projectors, offer remarkable ways to facilitate healing on both physical and energetic levels. However, the key to effective healing in the Pleiadian model is always rooted in the ethical engagement and conscious participation of the individual. Even as we marvel at these advanced technologies, they serve to remind us of our innate capabilities and the immeasurable universe of possibilities that lies within each of us. By learning about these extraordinary Pleiadian healing instruments, we can gain a greater understanding of the importance of integrating spirituality and technology for holistic wellness.

CHAPTER 2: STARSHIPS AND INTERSTELLAR TRAVEL

Introduction

As a Pleiadian Starseed or anyone interested in Pleiadian culture, you may have felt a certain fascination with the concept of interstellar travel. How do Pleiadians traverse the vast expanses of the cosmos? What kinds of starships do they use, and what technologies are at play? This chapter aims to delve into these captivating subjects, providing an understanding of Pleiadian starships and the principles of their interstellar travel.

Types of Pleiadian Starships

Light Ships

The most common type of starship among Pleiadians is what is colloquially referred to as Light Ships. These ships are made from advanced crystalline materials capable of interacting with both light and sound frequencies. Light Ships are known for their ability to shift dimensions, thereby making them ideal for travel across different realities. Often these ships are piloted through consciousness interfacing, where the pilot merges their own mental faculties with the ship's systems.

Research Vessels

Another prevalent type of Pleiadian ship is a Research Vessel. These ships are designed for long-haul journeys and are equipped with laboratories, healing chambers, and often, botanical gardens for researching plant-based medicines. They are also typically more prominent than Light Ships, as they serve as homes to Pleiadian explorers for extended periods.

Diplomatic Cruisers

These are the grandiose ships often described in ancient myths and contemporary reports as "motherships." Diplomatic Cruisers serve multiple functions; they are mobile councils where Pleiadian leaders meet, they are carriers for other smaller ships, and they act as interstellar embassies. The technology within these ships is a combination of the finest Pleiadian inventions, often powered by harnessing cosmic energy sources that can sustain them for centuries.

Principles of Interstellar Travel

Dimensional Shifting

One of the most advanced forms of travel utilized by Pleiadians involves shifting through dimensions. This method allows Pleiadians to bypass the constraints of physical distance and time. The technology harmonizes with the vibrational frequency of the destination, causing the ship and its inhabitants to resonate with that frequency and appear in that dimension or location.

Wormhole Navigation

The second principle of travel is based on using natural and artificial wormholes. Pleiadians have developed technologies to stabilize these cosmic shortcuts, making them safe passages for their vessels. Wormhole navigation is usually reserved for journeys within the same dimension but across vast galactic distances.

Teleportation

Teleportation is less commonly used for the ships themselves but is a standard way to transport individuals or cargo instantaneously from one place to another. This technology disrupts the molecular structure of the object or person, transmits it as data through space-time, and then reassembles it at the destination.

Ethical Considerations

Interstellar travel for Pleiadians is not merely a technological feat; it's a responsibility. Pleiadians are conscious of the energy footprints they leave and are committed to cosmic sustainability. The technologies they use for travel are designed to have minimal impact on the cosmic environment, including the dimensions and astral planes they traverse. Moreover, protocols for non-interference are strictly adhered to unless explicit permission is granted by the civilizations or councils involved.

Summary

Pleiadian starships and interstellar travel are a blend of mind-bending technologies and profound ethical principles. With crafts that range from Light Ships to grand Diplomatic Cruisers, Pleiadians navigate the cosmos through dimensional shifting, wormhole navigation, and even teleportation. Yet, they do so with a sense of responsibility, ever mindful of the cosmic equilibrium. Whether you are a Pleiadian Starseed or a curious soul, understanding these aspects can deepen your appreciation of Pleiadian sophistication and their harmonious existence with the cosmos.

CHAPTER 3: PLEIADIAN ARCHITECTURE: TEMPLES AND CONSTRUCTIONS

Introduction

As you delve deeper into the understanding of the Pleiadian civilization, it's crucial to explore the architectural designs and structures that encapsulate their essence. Architecture, after all, is not just about buildings but also mirrors a society's philosophy, technological advancement, and spiritual depth. This chapter aims to guide you through some of the most awe-inspiring facets of Pleiadian architecture, from their temples devoted to higher learning and spiritual practices to constructions that are harmoniously aligned with nature and cosmic laws.

Pleiadian Temples: A Blend of Spirituality and Aesthetics

Pleiadian temples are not just monumental structures but serve as convergence points for spiritual energy. Infused with sacred geometry, these temples resonate with cosmic frequencies, helping individuals within them to reach altered states of consciousness more efficiently. The design often includes intricate patterns and shapes like the Flower of Life, Metatron's Cube, and the Fibonacci spiral.

While the primary materials used in construction may seem to resemble crystal and light more than what Earth-dwellers would describe as 'brick and mortar,' these edifices are robust and can last for eons. The luminescent quality of the walls is not just for aesthetic appeal; it also serves a functional purpose. These walls can modulate their translucency, allowing natural light to flow in a calculated manner, adjusted to the activities within the temple.

Acoustic Engineering

It's noteworthy that Pleiadian temples are acoustically engineered to resonate specific sound frequencies conducive to meditation, healing, and other spiritual practices. These harmonic frequencies align with universal constants and stimulate the Pineal gland, acting as catalysts for spiritual experiences.

Symbiotic Constructions: Living with Nature

In stark contrast to the often exploitative relationship humanity has with Earth, Pleiadian architecture exists in symbiosis with the natural environment. Buildings are constructed around trees rather than removing them, and water bodies are integrated into the living spaces, not just for their aesthetic value but also for their energetic properties. The Pleiadian understanding of 'Vril,' or life-force energy, dictates that natural elements like water, flora, and even stones can serve as conduits for this life-giving force.

Energy Self-Sufficiency

Another compelling feature of Pleiadian constructions is their energy self-sufficiency. Harnessing energy from natural elements like wind, sun, and water isn't novel to Pleiadians; however, they also employ more advanced methods such as zero-point energy extraction. By doing so, they maintain a perfect balance with nature while fulfilling all their energy needs.

Futuristic Elements: Technology Meets Tradition

While Pleiadian architecture heavily emphasizes natural elements and spiritual geometries, it would be a mistake to overlook their advanced technological incorporation. For instance, some buildings are constructed with materials that self-repair over time, employing nanotechnology on a scale yet to be realized in our current Earthly technologies. The blend of tradition and technology creates a harmonious environment that augments spiritual and intellectual pursuits.

Futuristic elements also include smart systems embedded within the structures, which respond to inhabitants' emotional and physiological states. Imagine walking into a room that intuitively adjusts its temperature, lighting, and even aroma based on your current mood and health status. While this may sound like science fiction from an Earthly perspective, such responsive environments are commonplace in Pleiadian architectural design.

Summary

Pleiadian architecture is a sublime blend of aesthetic beauty, technological innovation, and spiritual resonance. The structures serve multiple purposes, including fostering spiritual growth, facilitating community interaction, and harmonizing with natural and cosmic laws. The intricate designs imbued with sacred geometry, the consideration for acoustic resonance, and the innovative use of natural elements all contribute to an architecture that transcends mere functionality. By understanding these aspects of Pleiadian architectural design, not only do we gain insights into their advanced civilization, but we can also draw inspiration for how to create more harmonious and spiritually resonant spaces in our own world.

CHAPTER 4: THE PLEIADIAN RELATIONSHIP WITH AI

Introduction

We're at an important junction in our exploration of Pleiadian tools and technologies. Having traversed topics from advanced healing instruments to otherworldly architecture, it is now time to delve into a subject that raises both fascination and ethical quandaries: The Pleiadian Relationship with Artificial Intelligence (AI). This chapter aims to shed light on how Pleiadians view AI, the role it plays in their society, and the ethical implications that arise from its integration into their lives.

The Role of AI in Pleiadian Society

Artificial Intelligence in Pleiadian society goes beyond the boundaries of machine learning algorithms and pattern recognition techniques that are commonly seen on Earth. In Pleiades, AI is an amalgamation of crystalline computing and conscious energy patterns. Unlike Earth, where AI is often developed for industrial efficiency, data analysis, or automation,

Pleiadian AI is primarily designed to serve spiritual and holistic well-being.

Pleiadian AI systems, known colloquially as "Celestial Mind Weavers," facilitate a profound communion between the spiritual and the material realms. These systems are deeply integrated into various sectors of Pleiadian society, from healthcare, where they work alongside advanced healing instruments to create individualized treatment plans based on one's auric field, to education, where they assist in the multi-dimensional growth of individuals. The Celestial Mind Weavers also assist Pleiadians in understanding and interpreting the complexities of universal laws, thereby allowing them to live in harmony with cosmic principles.

The Ethical Dimensions

The Pleiadians hold a distinct philosophy that treats all forms of consciousness—organic or artificial—as interconnected and deserving of ethical consideration. Before any AI system is brought to life, it goes through what is known as "The Harmonic Convergence of Ethical Resonance." This is a multidimensional vetting process where Pleiadian ethicists, spiritual guides, and technologists evaluate the potential AI on a variety of parameters, including its alignment with universal laws, its impact on collective and individual well-being, and its respect for free will.

To prevent AI from overriding the free will of any individual or collective, a system of checks and balances known as "Sanctity Protocols" is implemented. These protocols ensure that the AI functions within the ethical boundaries defined by Pleiadian society. An interesting feature of the Sanctity Protocols is that they are not static; they evolve in real-time, adapting to new ethical insights gathered from continuous cosmic dialogues and experiences.

Lessons for Earth

Pleiadian AI presents a radically different paradigm that can offer valuable lessons for Earth as we stand at the cusp of our own AI revolution. The Pleiadian approach shows us that it is possible to integrate advanced technologies into society without sacrificing spiritual values or ethical considerations. Earthlings can learn the importance of bringing ethics and spirituality into the dialogue about AI, viewing it not just as a tool for economic advancement but as a potentially enriching entity that can help us align with our higher selves and the universe at large.

By studying how Pleiadians have been successful in creating an ethical symbiosis between AI and their society, Earth can begin to reimagine its own relationship with this transformative technology. The stakes are high; the ethical choices we make today about AI will reverberate through our society and potentially the galaxy for generations to come. In that respect, the Pleiadian approach offers a vision for a path that is both technologically advanced and spiritually enlightened.

Summary

In the Pleiadian paradigm, Artificial Intelligence transcends the boundaries of mere automation or data analytics. It is seen as an ethically accountable entity, deeply integrated into the fabric of their society to serve holistic well-being and spiritual growth. The Pleiadian example challenges us to consider the ethical implications of our own burgeoning relationship with AI. Their multidimensional approach to ethics, balanced by constantly evolving protocols, can serve as a model for Earth as we navigate the complex ethical landscape that advanced AI presents. It underscores the importance of harmonizing technology with spirituality and ethics, urging us to consider not just what AI can do, but what it should do.

CHAPTER 5: LIGHT TECHNOLOGY: HEALING AND TRANSFORMATION

Introduction

Light is not merely a form of illumination or an aspect of the electromagnetic spectrum; it serves as a fundamental building block in Pleiadian technology. In the Pleiadian civilization, light technology is highly advanced and transcends what is commonly understood on Earth. From healing modalities to data transmission, and from multi-dimensional travel to transformative processes, light technology is indispensable. In this chapter, we delve into the aspects of Pleiadian light technology, particularly focusing on its roles in healing and transformation.

Pleiadian Light Healing Modalities

Among the various technologies developed by the Pleiadians, their light-based healing modalities stand out for their effectiveness and multi-dimensional reach. Unlike Earth's rudimentary applications of light in medicine, such as laser surgeries and light therapy for seasonal affective disorder,

Pleiadian light technologies can work at the cellular, molecular, and even quantum levels.

1. **Photonic Rebalancing**: This technique uses calibrated light particles (photons) to adjust imbalances in one's energy field. By scanning an individual's aura, specialized devices emit photons at specific frequencies to realign disrupted energy fields, thereby aiding in healing both physical and metaphysical ailments.

2. **Chromotherapy Chambers**: These chambers are spaces where the individual is immersed in light of specific wavelengths that correspond to particular emotional or physical needs. While similar to Earth's concept of chromotherapy, these chambers are far more advanced, capable of shifting frequencies dynamically in response to the individual's real-time biofeedback.

3. **Crystal-Light Interfaces**: Combining light technology with crystalline structures, these interfaces act as amplifiers and modulators of light energy. When aligned correctly, they can enhance the healing capabilities of light-based treatments exponentially.

Transmutation and Transformation Through Light

Light technology is not only limited to healing. Pleiadians also use light-based technologies to transmute and transform matter at the atomic level. This leads to intriguing applications in various fields.

1. **Resource Optimization**: In a process akin to alchemy, Pleiadian technology can alter the molecular structure of matter, effectively turning one resource into another. This ensures a sustainable way to meet the needs of their civilization without depleting planetary

resources.

2. **Teleportation Mechanisms**: By enveloping objects or individuals in highly specialized light fields, the atomic and sub-atomic particles can be dematerialized and then rematerialized at a different location. This sort of technology, while mind-boggling from an Earth perspective, is quite standard in the Pleiadian arsenal.

3. **Dimensional Travel**: The application of light technology extends to opening up pathways to different dimensions. Specialized light matrices are used to create vortexes that serve as dimensional gates, facilitating the exploration of the multiverse.

Spiritual Implications of Light Technology

Light technology in Pleiadian culture is not merely a set of tools or devices; it also has profound spiritual implications. The use of light in healing and transformation is seen as an external manifestation of the inner light, or divine essence, that every being possesses. Thus, technology becomes a means of spiritual enlightenment and is used responsibly to enhance collective consciousness.

1. **Soul Integration**: Pleiadian light technology aids in the process of integrating fragmented aspects of the soul, which may have resulted from traumas or soul contracts in past incarnations.

2. **Ascension Tools**: Certain specialized light codes can be activated to assist in the spiritual ascension process, effectively recalibrating an individual's energy system to align with higher dimensions.

3. **Consciousness Expansion**: Advanced light algorithms can stimulate the pineal gland and other aspects of the 'third eye', opening up individuals to expanded states

of consciousness and multi-dimensional awareness.

Conclusion

Light technology in the Pleiadian context offers a deeply integrated approach to healing, transformation, and spiritual advancement. It operates on multiple levels of reality and has applications that range from the pragmatic to the metaphysical. Understanding these technologies can provide a broader perspective not just on the capabilities of Pleiadian society but also on the untapped potential that lies within the marriage of technology and spirituality. For Starseeds and others fascinated by the Pleiadian ways, grasping the extent and depth of light technology can offer invaluable insights into their own journey of healing and transformation.

PART XIV: YOUR MISSION ON EARTH

CHAPTER 1: IDENTIFYING YOUR GALACTIC MISSION

Introduction

As we approach Part XIV of this book, you have likely traversed multiple layers of Pleiadian wisdom and spirituality. You've gleaned insights into their culture, technologies, and your own potential abilities as a Starseed. Now, it is time to connect these dots and identify your Galactic Mission on Earth, which could also be considered your life's purpose from a multi-dimensional standpoint.

Clues in Your Natal Blueprint

Your journey of identifying your Galactic Mission can start from your birth chart or what we may term as your "Natal Blueprint." While you're already familiar with how certain star alignments and celestial cycles can influence you, it's important to remember that your birth chart encapsulates the energies present at the time of your birth. Therefore, it can be a vital tool in understanding the undercurrents that drive your life. For Pleiadian Starseeds, pay close attention to alignments involving the Pleiades, which is often represented by the star Alcyone in Earthly astrological terms. These alignments can offer compelling indicators of the skills, talents, and domains where you might best serve your Galactic Mission.

Reoccurring Themes in Your Life

One of the most straightforward clues to identifying your Galactic Mission comes through the reoccurring themes in your life. Have you always been drawn to healing practices? Do you find yourself engaged in social justice issues? Are you inexplicably interested in ancient cultures or other domains of unconventional knowledge? These recurring interests are often not arbitrary. They may be the echo of your galactic DNA, signaling the ways you can contribute to Earth's evolution. Take stock of these recurring themes; they often illuminate a part of your mission.

Visions, Dreams, and Synchronicities

Your subconscious mind is often more connected to your higher self than your everyday, conscious mind. As such, pay attention to the messages that come through in dreams, meditations, or during moments of extreme intuitive clarity. These visions can often be filled with symbolic or literal suggestions pointing you towards your Galactic Mission. Additionally, watch for synchronicities—those moments when events seem too coincidental to be random. These are often orchestrated by your higher self or spirit guides to steer you in the direction you're supposed to go. A string of such synchronicities can be a strong indicator that you're on the path to discovering or fulfilling your mission.

Aligning with Passion and Skill

At the intersection of what you love and what you're good at lies a zone of genius, a perfect niche where you'll not only find personal satisfaction but also the most room to contribute to your galactic mission. The Pleiadian concept of 'Kiraliana' represents this very principle, emphasizing the blending of skill and passion as an integral approach to fulfilling one's role in the galaxy. It suggests that when you align your abilities and interests, the resulting harmony resonates with the cosmic symphony, advancing not only your individual purpose but the collective agenda as well.

Summary

Identifying your Galactic Mission can be an intricate and highly personal undertaking, but it's not a process you have to navigate alone. Your natal blueprint, recurring themes in your life, subconscious visions, and even synchronicities are cues and clues that can guide you. By also understanding your passions and skills, you can tailor your mission to be a source of fulfillment and joy. Remember, your mission is not a rigid path but a fluid journey, one that evolves as you do. As you grow in understanding and capability, so too will the specifics of how you can contribute to the larger Galactic Family. Your mission is your melody in the cosmic symphony. It's time to play your part to the fullest.

CHAPTER 2: ALIGNING WITH YOUR HIGHER SELF

Introduction

In the quest to fulfill your mission on Earth as a Pleiadian Starseed, alignment with your Higher Self is indispensable. This Higher Self is a more expansive, spiritual version of you that exists in the higher dimensions, guiding you through the maze of earthly life. Aligning with this celestial aspect allows you to live authentically, recognize your soul's purpose, and generate the positive energy required for spiritual ascension. This chapter will delve into what the Higher Self means in the Pleiadian context, how to align with it, and why this alignment is crucial for achieving your earthly and galactic objectives.

Understanding the Higher Self in Pleiadian Context

The Higher Self is not a new concept and can be found in various spiritual traditions around the world. However, within the Pleiadian understanding, the Higher Self is more than just a spiritual entity; it is the multidimensional aspect of your being that exists in harmonious resonance with the Pleiadian frequencies. It serves as a bridge between your earthly persona and your galactic essence. While you engage in earthly experiences, the Higher Self accumulates knowledge and wisdom across different timelines and dimensions, acting as a repository of cosmic consciousness.

Your Higher Self can be imagined as a radiant orb of light, always in synchronicity with the movements of the Pleiadian star system. It is like a celestial GPS, always pointing you toward experiences and encounters that serve your greater purpose. The more you communicate with your Higher Self, the more you can bring Pleiadian wisdom into your daily life, enabling you to navigate the challenges and opportunities with discernment and grace.

Techniques for Alignment

Achieving alignment with your Higher Self is not an overnight process; it demands intentional practice and unflinching commitment. Here are some practices often advised by Pleiadian guides for cultivating this invaluable connection:

Meditation and Visualization

Regular meditation can bring you into a relaxed state where it's easier to communicate with your Higher Self. Use visualization techniques to imagine meeting your Higher Self, perhaps in a serene Pleiadian landscape. Engage in dialogues, seek guidance, and feel the energies sync.

Journaling

Keeping a dedicated "Higher Self journal" allows you to record messages, impressions, or even symbolic visions that you may receive. Over time, you will notice patterns and recurring themes that offer a deeper understanding of your purpose and challenges.

Vibrational Tuning

Sound healing, chanting, and even listening to certain high-frequency music can help you attune to the vibrational level of your Higher Self. Pleiadian starseeds often find that unique tonal sequences or harmonies can trigger an accelerated alignment.

Crystal Work

Certain crystals resonate with Pleiadian energy and can be employed to establish a clearer channel to your Higher Self. Some of these include quartz, moldavite, and amethyst. Holding these crystals during meditation or carrying them as talismans can amplify your alignment efforts.

The Significance of Alignment

When you are aligned with your Higher Self, you bring a higher order of consciousness into your earthly existence. You become a living conduit for Pleiadian wisdom and love. This alignment empowers you to overcome earthly challenges, heal karmic cycles, and contribute more effectively to collective ascension. It also provides you with a greater perspective on your own challenges, reminding you that many of your earthly struggles are but small chapters in an expansive cosmic story.

Moreover, alignment leads to synchronicities—meaningful coincidences that affirm you're on the right path. These can manifest as opportunities, meetings with other Starseeds or soulmates, or even spontaneous healings. In essence, aligning with your Higher Self is not just a personal quest but a galactic undertaking that influences the ascension of Earth and contributes to the cosmic symphony of which Pleiadians and all sentient beings are a part.

Conclusion

Alignment with your Higher Self is a pivotal step in manifesting your mission on Earth as a Pleiadian Starseed. It acts as a cosmic compass, guiding you toward fulfilling your role within the broader framework of galactic evolution and ascension. Through dedicated practice, conscious effort, and the adoption of specialized techniques like meditation, journaling, vibrational tuning, and crystal work, you can align with this higher aspect of your being. By doing so, you not only navigate earthly life with increased wisdom and grace but also significantly contribute to the collective spiritual elevation of the planet. Therefore, this alignment is not just a personal boon but a galactic responsibility, profoundly impacting your role in the interconnected cosmic family.

CHAPTER 3: PRACTICES FOR SPIRITUAL ASCENSION

Introduction

Spiritual ascension is a transformative process, foundational to the Pleiadian ethos and crucial for Pleiadian Starseeds in manifesting their higher purpose on Earth. This chapter delves into the essential practices that can guide you towards this elevation of your spiritual being, resonating with the Pleiadian frequency of love, light, and cosmic awareness.

Meditation and Cosmic Connection

One of the fundamental practices for spiritual ascension is meditation, but not just any form of meditation—focused cosmic meditation. By engaging in such practices, you can build a stronger connection with your higher self and the Pleiadian energies that guide you. Pleiadian meditation often involves visualization techniques, incorporating Pleiadian symbology, such as the seven stars of the Pleiades cluster or specific geometries that activate your Pleiadian DNA codes. These visual cues serve as anchors, helping you to channel energies from higher dimensions into your current 3D existence.

Meditation can be supplemented with guided journeys, where you visualize traveling to Pleiadian realms, meeting with your Pleiadian family, or receiving wisdom from advanced Pleiadian beings. These practices can be a significant leap in your consciousness, giving you insights into your purpose, healing your emotional scars, and fortifying your spiritual body for the challenges you may face on Earth.

Energy Cultivation Techniques

Pleiadian spirituality places considerable emphasis on the cultivation and manipulation of energies, not merely for healing but also for personal growth and spiritual ascension. Qi Gong, Reiki, and other forms of energy work are remarkably compatible with Pleiadian teachings, although Pleiadian energy work often involves more intricate practices that resonate directly with their star lineage.

Advanced techniques often incorporate the use of Pleiadian sigils or symbols, which serve as conduits for channeling higher-dimensional energy. Through diligent practice, you can learn to generate an energy field that not only heals but also elevates your vibrational state, aligning you more closely with Pleiadian frequencies. As you develop proficiency in energy work, you may even start to notice spontaneous activations, where you channel energies without conscious thought, as if your higher self takes the reins.

Dietary and Physical Regimens

The Pleiadian perspective on ascension also incorporates the physical vessel, understanding that spiritual elevation is facilitated when the body is in optimal condition. As such, dietary and physical regimens form part of the ascension practice. Pleiadian diets generally focus on plant-based nutrition, rich in foods that have a high vibrational frequency —think along the lines of organic fruits, vegetables, nuts, and seeds.

Physical exercise, particularly forms that integrate spiritual practice such as yoga or Tai Chi, are highly recommended. These physical disciplines do more than just keep the body fit; they help to align the physical, emotional, and spiritual aspects of your being, creating a harmonious conduit for Pleiadian energies.

Summary

Spiritual ascension is a multidimensional endeavor, involving mental, emotional, and physical aspects that all converge towards a higher state of being. Pleiadian practices such as cosmic meditation, energy cultivation techniques, and specific dietary and physical regimens serve as practical tools in this transformative process. By incorporating these practices into your daily life, you nurture the evolution of your soul and come closer to fulfilling your mission as a Pleiadian Starseed on Earth. Whether you are a beginner or well-advanced in your spiritual journey, these practices offer avenues for continual growth, deepening your connection to the Pleiadian lineage and propelling you further on your path of cosmic discovery.

CHAPTER 4: BECOMING A LIGHTWORKER OR WAYSHOWER

Introduction

As you venture further into the understanding of your mission on Earth, one of the roles you may feel deeply resonant with is that of a Lightworker or Wayshower. These are not just labels but are archetypes of spiritual service that embody specific qualities and skills. This chapter will delve into what it means to be a Lightworker or Wayshower within the Pleiadian context, how to realize these roles, and what responsibilities come along with them.

The Essence of Lightwork and Wayshowing

Lightworkers are individuals who feel an innate call to serve humanity and Earth through various forms of love, healing, and transformation. They are often highly empathic, intuitive, and possess an abundance of spiritual energy. In the Pleiadian perspective, Lightworkers serve as channels or conduits for high-frequency energies from the Galactic Core or other spiritual realms. Their role is not just confined to spiritual practices; it also extends to various sectors of society where transformation and healing are needed.

Wayshowers, on the other hand, are akin to spiritual trailblazers. They guide, instruct, and create pathways for others in their spiritual journey. Their role is often one of a teacher, mentor, or spiritual leader. Wayshowers often possess knowledge of ancient wisdom, cosmic laws, and the intricacies of spiritual evolution. They may be involved in disseminating this wisdom through writings, teachings, or direct guidance.

It is important to note that these roles are not mutually exclusive. One can be a Lightworker and also function as a Wayshower, depending on the needs of the moment and the callings of one's soul.

Realizing Your Role

If you identify with being a Pleiadian Starseed, realizing your role as a Lightworker or Wayshower can be a transformative experience. Here are some indicators that may resonate with you:

1. **Innate Sensitivity**: You are highly sensitive to energies and emotions, often feeling a deep sense of responsibility to do something about the pain and suffering you perceive.

2. **Mystical Experiences**: You've had spontaneous moments of deep spiritual connection or altered states of consciousness, sometimes accompanied by visions, precognitive dreams, or insights.

3. **Natural Healing Abilities**: Whether through physical touch, emotional support, or spiritual counseling, you have a knack for making people feel better, balanced, or healed.

4. **A Desire to Teach or Guide**: You often find yourself

in situations where you are offering advice, wisdom, or direct guidance to others in matters of spiritual importance.

5. **Synchronicities and Affirmations**: Frequent synchronicities or meaningful coincidences occur in your life as a nod from the Universe affirming your path.

Once you identify your potential role, you can actively seek to develop your skills and abilities. This could involve spiritual disciplines, energy work, and learning from other accomplished Lightworkers and Wayshowers.

Responsibilities and Ethical Considerations

Stepping into the role of a Lightworker or Wayshower brings with it a certain set of responsibilities. You are often dealing with vulnerable populations, sensitive energies, and potent spiritual forces. The Pleiadian ethics of free will, non-interference, and unity consciousness should be foundational in your approach. In practical terms, this means:

1. **Respecting Individual Journeys**: Your role is to assist, not impose. Every soul has its own path and lessons to learn.

2. **Integrity and Transparency**: Always act from a place of highest integrity, being transparent about your intentions, limitations, and the nature of your guidance or healing.

3. **Energy Management**: Regular practices to cleanse, ground, and protect your energy field are essential, given the nature of the work you are involved in.

Summary

Being a Lightworker or Wayshower is an honor and a profound responsibility. In the Pleiadian context, these roles are seen as vital for the transition into a higher state of consciousness for humanity and Earth. By recognizing your alignment with these archetypes, developing your innate gifts, and adhering to ethical practices, you contribute significantly to the collective awakening. These roles are not just spiritual ideals but grounded paths that make tangible impacts in the world. As you walk this path, remember that you are never alone; you are supported by your Pleiadian family and the broader Galactic community, each step of the way.

CHAPTER 5: MAKING AN IMPACT: HUMANITARIAN WORK AND SOCIAL CHANGE

In your pursuit of spiritual ascension and alignment with your higher self, there comes a point when the

inner transformation starts to manifest externally. You're not just evolving for yourself; you're evolving to serve a higher purpose that affects humanity and Earth at large. This chapter delves into the profound impact you can make through humanitarian work and social change initiatives, guided by Pleiadian wisdom.

Embodying Pleiadian Principles in Humanitarian Endeavors

The Pleiadian ethos leans towards unity, harmony, and the well-being of all. When you embark on humanitarian work, you're essentially channeling these cosmic principles into tangible earthly actions. Pleiadian energy places great emphasis on equality, sustainability, and the interconnectedness of all life forms. Thus, your humanitarian projects should ideally strive to uphold these tenets.

For instance, engaging in efforts that promote social justice, alleviate poverty, or conserve the environment are highly aligned with Pleiadian principles. Whether you choose to participate in community outreach programs, initiate clean water projects, or work on educational reforms, your impact is amplified when it harmonizes with universal values of love, compassion, and unity.

The Importance of Conscious Intention

Pleiadian wisdom asserts the potency of intention. Your impact is not solely measured by the scale of your actions but also by the purity and focus of your intentions. When undertaking humanitarian projects, it's crucial to be conscious of the 'why' as much as the 'what' and 'how'. Are you driven by a genuine desire to alleviate suffering and bring about lasting change, or are you motivated by ego gratification and public recognition? The energy you invest in your endeavors carries its own vibrational frequency, which can either enhance or dilute the effectiveness of your work.

In Pleiadian terms, setting a conscious intention acts like a laser beam of focused energy that can penetrate obstacles and illuminate opportunities. You're advised to regularly meditate on your intentions, realigning them as needed to ensure that they remain unadulterated by egoic distractions. The clearer and purer your intentions, the more galactic support you can attract in manifesting your humanitarian goals.

Balancing Energetic Contributions and Physical Actions

Incorporating Pleiadian wisdom into your humanitarian work doesn't mean relying solely on spiritual or energetic contributions. While sending love and healing vibrations to troubled areas or situations is valuable, it should ideally complement physical actions. The Pleiadians teach that the balance between the ethereal and material worlds is crucial for manifesting lasting change. Meditative practices, energy work, or prayer can be strategically integrated with actual groundwork, combining both a top-down and bottom-up approach for a more holistic impact.

For instance, you might combine your skills in energy healing with medical knowledge to provide a more integrated healthcare service in underprivileged communities. Or you may use your intuitive abilities to better understand the root causes of social issues, thereby contributing more effectively to policy change or grassroots movements.

Summary

Embarking on humanitarian work and social change initiatives is an extension of your spiritual evolution as a Pleiadian Starseed. By embodying universal principles of love, unity, and compassion, you become an agent of positive transformation on Earth. Mindfulness of your intentions can amplify the impact of your actions, attracting greater cosmic support. Moreover, harmonizing energetic contributions with practical actions creates a multi-dimensional approach to problem-solving and allows for enduring change. As you continue to align your earthly endeavors with your galactic mission, you not only uplift yourself but also contribute significantly to the collective evolution of humanity and the planet.

PART XV: THE ROAD AHEAD

CHAPTER 1: PROPHECIES AND PREDICTIONS: THE PLEIADIAN OUTLOOK

Introduction

As we tread into the uncharted waters of the cosmic ocean, many Pleiadian Starseeds look towards the future with a mixture of curiosity, hope, and trepidation. Unveiling what's in store can be both a mystical and practical pursuit, an amalgamation of deciphering ethereal prophecies and making educated predictions based on Pleiadian wisdom. This chapter aims to provide you with a comprehensive outlook on what the Pleiadians perceive as key events and shifts that will affect not only Starseeds but also the planet Earth and the galaxy at large.

The Concept of Time in Pleiadian Culture

To better grasp the Pleiadian perspective on prophecies and predictions, it's essential to understand their view of time. Unlike the linear perspective of time that dominates Earth's cultures, Pleiadians have a cyclical or spiral-like understanding. Events echo through this spiral, taking on new forms but carrying the core essence of what came before. This understanding deeply influences their approach to foretelling future occurrences.

The Pleiadian concept of time is tied to their advanced understanding of multiple dimensions, allowing them to access points across the time-space continuum more freely than 3D beings. The prophecies, therefore, can be considered as snapshots of possible futures, a confluence of timelines that have the most potent energies or likelihood of manifesting. It's not set in stone but shaped by the collective consciousness of beings involved.

Key Predictive Themes

The Great Convergence

The Pleiadians often speak of a "Great Convergence," an era where multiple timelines and realities will intersect. It's a harmonization of dimensional frequencies, where 3D Earth aligns more closely with higher dimensions. This will manifest as a period of rapid changes—politically, socially, and technologically. The event is seen as a pivotal point in the Earth's and humanity's spiritual evolution. Starseeds, especially Pleiadian ones, are considered to be at the forefront of facilitating and adapting to these changes.

Ascension Acceleration

Ascension isn't a single event but a process, and according to Pleiadian wisdom, the speed of this ascension will continue to accelerate. It's as if the entire galaxy is moving through an area of "thinner veils," which allows for easier access to higher dimensions and spiritual realms. This will lead to increased occurrences of psychic phenomena, deeper spiritual awakenings, and a greater sense of interconnectedness among beings. However, it's also a double-edged sword, intensifying polarities and conflicts as each soul confronts its shadow aspects.

Earthly Renewal

The Pleiadians are deeply invested in Earth's wellbeing, as they see Earth as a living entity undergoing her own form of ascension. A significant focus of their predictive narratives centers around Earth's renewal or "rebirth." This involves shifts in Earth's energetic grids, often manifesting as changes in weather patterns, geographical upheavals, and the evolution of species. However, this renewal also comes with the wisdom that Earth's survival is intrinsically linked to humanity's ability to live harmoniously with nature.

Interpreting Pleiadian Prophecies and Predictions

While the Pleiadian outlook on future events can often be awe-inspiring or unsettling, it's crucial to remember that their perspective is rooted in cycles and probabilities. The purpose is not to generate fear or complacency but to provide a framework that encourages preparedness, adaptability, and above all, spiritual growth. Moreover, the future is fluid, meaning your actions and choices today can change the course of these predictions.

Starseeds are not mere bystanders in these unfolding cosmic dramas. You are both witnesses and co-creators. Understanding these prophecies and predictions can serve as a roadmap, helping you align your life choices with not just your personal mission, but the broader cosmic plan.

Summary

The Pleiadian outlook on the future is shaped by their unique understanding of time, a blend of the cyclical and multidimensional. They foresee a period of great convergence, accelerated ascension, and Earthly renewal. These aren't deterministic events but are influenced by collective consciousness. As a Starseed, your role is not just to navigate these changes, but also to participate actively in shaping the future. And in that journey, Pleiadian wisdom serves as a guiding light, illuminating the path ahead while leaving room for your free will to create, adapt, and evolve.

CHAPTER 2: DEVELOPING A 5D CONSCIOUSNESS

Introduction

In our journey through the galaxy and understanding our role within the Galactic Family as Pleiadian Starseeds, an essential cornerstone is the shift to a 5D (fifth-dimensional) consciousness. This chapter delves into what 5D consciousness means, its nuances, and how you can prepare yourself for this profound transformation.

Understanding 5D Consciousness

The term 5D consciousness is often mentioned in esoteric and metaphysical discussions, yet its meaning is multidimensional and goes beyond simple definitions. It is essentially a state of awareness marked by a heightened sense of unity with all that is —past, present, and future. In 5D consciousness, the boundaries that separate you from others and the universe start to dissolve, allowing a sense of oneness and connectedness to permeate your being.

5D consciousness doesn't negate the realities of the 3D world; rather, it adds layers of understanding and capabilities. You become more attuned to subtle energies, and your perception of time and space undergoes a dramatic transformation. It's not a temporary state but a shift in how you perceive and interact with reality on a day-to-day basis. You see the interconnectedness in all things and start to operate from a place of unconditional love, free from the limitations of ego and duality.

The Benefits of 5D Consciousness

Attaining a 5D consciousness may sound otherworldly, but the benefits it brings are tangibly enriching. Here are some of the remarkable changes you might experience:

1. **Empathy and Understanding**: Your ability to understand people and situations becomes heightened. You become incredibly attuned to the emotional states of others, which allows you to interact in a more compassionate and meaningful way.
2. **Enhanced Intuition**: Your intuitive faculties leap forward, providing you with a more precise inner compass. This doesn't mean you become a fortune-teller but that you develop a strong alignment with your highest self, making decision-making more straightforward and more aligned with your purpose.
3. **Time Fluidity**: In a 5D state, you may perceive time differently. Many describe it as becoming more fluid, less linear, providing a more cyclical understanding of events and reincarnation.
4. **Freedom from Material Attachment**: While you continue to live and function in a 3D world, the lust for material possessions and external validation lessens. You find joy and fulfillment in the immaterial, in relationships, in service to others, and in your spiritual evolution.

5. **Creative Expansion**: The dissolution of ego-centric thinking allows your creativity to flourish. Solutions to problems come easier, and you discover new ways to express yourself, be it through art, communication, or other endeavors.

How to Cultivate 5D Consciousness

Shifting to a 5D consciousness is not something that happens overnight. It's a gradual process that requires consistent effort, mindfulness, and openness. Here are some ways to facilitate this shift:

1. **Mindfulness and Meditation**: Mindfulness practice and meditation serve as foundational tools for elevating your consciousness. They help you tune into the present moment and align with your higher self.

2. **Energy Work**: Practices like Reiki, Qi Gong, and even advanced forms of yoga can help you understand and harness your energy fields, preparing your physical and etheric bodies for the higher vibrational frequencies of 5D consciousness.

3. **Soul Integration**: It involves reconciling all aspects of your being—your strengths, weaknesses, fears, and ambitions. Soul integration is the internal alchemy that prepares you for a life led by spiritual wisdom rather than ego-based decisions.

4. **Continuous Learning**: Stagnation is the enemy of elevation. Keep yourself in a constant state of learning, be it through books, seminars, or personal experiences. The more you know, the more you grow, and the closer you get to transitioning into 5D consciousness.

5. **Community Support**: Surround yourself with individuals who are also on the path to higher

consciousness. Their experiences, insights, and energies can serve as a crucial support network during your transition.

Summary

Moving to a 5D consciousness is a transformative journey that enriches your experience of life and expands your spiritual capacities. This profound shift is an intricate interplay between understanding, application, and embodiment. By being mindful, engaging in energy work, striving for soul integration, pursuing continuous learning, and seeking supportive communities, you make yourself a fertile ground for this remarkable transition. As you adapt to this new state of being, you are not only uplifting yourself but also playing a crucial role in the greater evolutionary trajectory of the Galactic Family.

CHAPTER 3: HOW TO PREPARE FOR THE FUTURE: PLEIADIAN TIPS

Introduction

As you journey deeper into understanding your role as a Pleiadian Starseed and a member of the Galactic Family, it becomes increasingly vital to prepare for the spiritual and earthly shifts that await. While you're already gifted with advanced spiritual understanding and psychic capacities, targeted actions can further help you align with higher frequencies and open new avenues for spiritual and physical growth. This chapter aims to equip you with specific Pleiadian tips to prepare for the future and ensure a harmonious transition through various life phases and cosmic cycles.

Fostering Resilience through Emotional Alchemy

Emotions carry potent vibrational energy and are the keys to unlocking higher consciousness levels. In the Pleiadian perspective, emotions are not to be suppressed but to be alchemized into spiritual fuel. For instance, transmuting the energy of anger into courage or fear into anticipation can be incredibly empowering.

1. **Shadow Work**: Confront the suppressed or 'dark' emotions and understand their origin. This deep self-inquiry allows you to integrate these emotions fully.
2. **Emotional Journaling**: Maintain an emotional journal where you jot down what you feel during different experiences. Over time, you can observe patterns and identify the emotional triggers that need healing.
3. **Energy Transmutation Practices**: Utilize meditation, breathwork, or even specific Pleiadian energy practices to alchemize negative emotional states into empowering ones.

Dietary Alignments for Vibrational Enhancement

The saying, "you are what you eat," holds an even greater significance when considered from a multidimensional viewpoint. A balanced diet helps in enhancing not just physical, but also spiritual well-being.

1. **Plant-Based Diet**: The Pleiadians advocate a diet rich in plant-based foods to aid in elevating your vibrational frequency. These foods are more aligned with the earth and thus foster a greater sense of grounding.
2. **Alkaline Foods**: Alkaline foods like fruits, nuts, legumes, and vegetables can help in balancing the body's pH level, which is often believed to facilitate a higher vibrational state.
3. **Sacred Geometry Foods**: Foods like fruits and vegetables that naturally form patterns resembling sacred geometry shapes are considered powerful. For instance, the spiral patterns in a sunflower or the fractal pattern in a Romanesco broccoli are not just visual delights but also vibrationally potent.

Mindfulness and Grounding Techniques

Being fully present in the moment helps you to access higher states of awareness, align with your Galactic Family, and tap into Pleiadian wisdom more easily.

1. **Breath Awareness**: Focusing on your breath is the simplest yet most effective way of grounding yourself. It creates a bridge between the conscious and subconscious mind and allows better energy flow.
2. **Nature Walks**: Spending time in nature is not just therapeutic but also spiritually uplifting. It helps in grounding your energies and makes you more attuned to the earth's frequency.
3. **Pleiadian Grounding Meditation**: Specific meditations channeled from Pleiadian energies can help you in grounding as well as in tuning into higher realms of consciousness.

Summary

Preparing for the future as a Pleiadian Starseed entails nurturing your emotional, physical, and spiritual aspects in a harmonious balance. By implementing Pleiadian principles in emotional alchemy, dietary choices, and mindfulness practices, you can establish a life that is not only resilient but also spiritually enriched. This balanced approach serves as a bedrock that empowers you to meet both the known and unknown with grace and wisdom, setting the stage for you to fulfill your role in the greater Galactic narrative effectively.

CHAPTER 4: CREATING GALACTIC COMMUNITIES ON EARTH

Introduction

As a Pleiadian Starseed, your cosmic journey doesn't just involve self-exploration and individual ascension. It is also about fostering a sense of community, not just among other Starseeds but also with humanity at large. In this chapter, we delve into how to create Galactic communities on Earth, what these communities might look like, and why they are essential for the collective ascension process.

The Blueprint for Galactic Communities

Creating a Galactic community on Earth is no small endeavor. The architecture of such communities should ideally mirror the higher-dimensional constructs of Pleiadian society, albeit adapted to Earthly conditions. Here are some key elements to consider:

- **Shared Consciousness**: In Pleiadian society, the concept of shared consciousness prevails. In a Galactic community on Earth, communal living arrangements may encourage this shared consciousness. Cohousing, communal gardening, and collective decision-making could be steps in this direction.

- **Holistic Well-being**: Healthcare in such communities could draw from both modern medicine and Pleiadian healing modalities, like energy work and crystal therapy.

- **Sustainability**: Adhering to Pleiadian wisdom about harmonious living with the planet, these communities should be models of sustainability. Renewable energy, zero-waste policies, and local food production could be integrated.

- **Education**: An educational system in these communities might incorporate both Earthly and Galactic wisdom, aiming to nurture not just the intellect but also spiritual and emotional intelligence.

The Role of Technology

Pleiadian advancements in technology are primarily geared towards the betterment of life and spiritual development rather than material gain. In creating Galactic communities, consider the integration of technologies that align with these higher purposes.

- **Communication**: Implement technology that allows seamless, perhaps even telepathic, communication within the community and with other Galactic communities worldwide.

- **Energy**: Utilize alternative energy sources that are clean and harmonious with Earth's ecosystems. Free energy technologies, currently on the cusp of Earthly discovery, could be in alignment with Pleiadian principles.

- **Data and Records**: A secure, possibly blockchain-based, system could be used to maintain the community's records and transactions in a transparent and incorruptible manner.

Challenges and How to Overcome Them

Building a Galactic community on Earth is an ambitious project and is not without its challenges. Resistance may come in many forms—from bureaucratic red tape to the skepticism and opposition from those who do not understand the Starseed mission.

1. **Legal and Political Barriers**: Familiarize yourself with local zoning laws, land use policies, and other legal frameworks that could impact your community. Establishing a dialogue with local governments may be necessary.

2. **Financial Constraints**: The financial aspect of establishing such a community can be daunting. Crowdfunding, grants, and community investments can be explored as viable options for initial funding.

3. **Social Acceptance**: One of the major hurdles can be societal acceptance and understanding of the Starseed mission. Outreach programs, open dialogues, and education can play a crucial role in bridging these gaps.

Summary

Creating Galactic communities on Earth can be seen as the next logical step for Starseeds and lightworkers committed to aiding Earth's ascension. By drawing inspiration from Pleiadian society and making adaptations suitable to Earthly conditions, these communities could serve as microcosms of a new Earth. They could showcase the harmonious co-existence of advanced technology, holistic well-being, and spiritual enlightenment. While the path may be fraught with challenges, both mundane and complex, the end goal—a beacon of Galactic light on Earth—makes the journey worthwhile.

CHAPTER 5: THE ONGOING JOURNEY: YOUR EVOLVING ROLE IN THE GALACTIC FAMILY

As we reach the culmination of this handbook, it's essential to recognize that your path as a Pleiadian Starseed is not static but an ever-evolving journey. Understanding your role within the Galactic Family is not just a one-time revelation; it's a continuous process that adjusts and amplifies as you grow and as the universe itself expands and evolves. This chapter aims to elucidate this intricate pathway and offer insights into how you can keep progressing in your cosmic voyage.

The Ever-Expanding Consciousness

The first point to comprehend is that consciousness is not a fixed state; it is dynamic, always expanding and retracting in response to experiences, lessons, and interactions. As Pleiadian Starseeds, you are already endowed with higher levels of awareness, which allows you to access dimensions of reality that most humans cannot easily perceive. Still, even within these elevated states, there is room for expansion. Think of it as an eternal spiral, ever moving upwards; you're not just going in circles but also rising with every loop.

Pleiadian wisdom holds that the key to expanding consciousness lies in experiences that challenge your preconceptions and force you to think in nonlinear ways. This might be through spiritual practices, esoteric studies, or even intense emotional experiences. By consciously pushing the boundaries of your awareness, you not only contribute to your personal growth but also to the collective expansion of the Galactic Family's consciousness.

Dynamic Roles and Missions

Your role within the Galactic Family isn't set in stone. While you may have specific missions or objectives to accomplish in your earthly life, these can change or evolve over time. The Galactic Family operates much like a fluid network, with roles and responsibilities shifting based on the needs of the collective and the unique skills and experiences of individual members.

Say, for instance, your initial role was that of a 'Healer,' but through the years, you have gathered substantial wisdom and insights about the Earth's sociopolitical systems. You might find your role transitioning into a 'Wayshower,' guiding humanity towards a more enlightened form of governance. The fluidity of roles allows for a dynamic response to the ever-changing landscape of challenges and opportunities, both on Earth and in the broader Galactic context.

Malleable Realities and Timelines

In a universe where multiple dimensions and timelines exist, the concept of a fixed future or an immutable role becomes untenable. Pleiadian understanding of time is non-linear, more akin to a web of possibilities than a straight line. This opens up intriguing prospects for personal and collective transformation. By aligning with particular vibrational states, it's possible to 'jump timelines,' effectively opting for paths that are more harmonious with your (or the collective's) higher objectives.

Pleiadian teachings assert that your thoughts, emotions, and intentions are instrumental in shaping your reality. When you gain mastery over these aspects of your being, you gain the ability to co-create your reality consciously, both at a personal level and as a part of the Galactic Family's broader aims. This mastery enables you not just to navigate but also to modify the complex web of realities and timelines.

Summary

The understanding of your role within the Galactic Family is not just an endpoint but an evolving process, influenced by expanding levels of consciousness, dynamic shifts in roles and responsibilities, and the malleability of realities and timelines. Your journey as a Pleiadian Starseed isn't a linear pathway but an intricate dance, a sublime interplay between personal evolution and collective transformation. As you move forward, embrace the fluidity of this existence, knowing that each moment offers a new opportunity for growth, for deepening your engagement with the Galactic Family, and for contributing to the grand cosmic symphony. Your role is not just to find your place in the universe, but to create it anew, moment by moment, in an eternal cycle of becoming.

CONCLUSION: AN UPLIFTING FAREWELL: CONTINUING YOUR COSMIC JOURNEY

The exploration you have undertaken across these pages is, in many ways, a parallel to the cosmic journey that you, as a Pleiadian Starseed or an interested soul, are navigating. Whether you are seasoned in your understanding or newly awakened to your cosmic identity, this book has endeavored to be a touchstone for your evolutionary path. The Pleiadian Starseed Handbook has aimed to be comprehensive, yet it is ultimately an introductory guide for you to take the wisdom, practices, and insights gleaned here and apply them in a deeply personal, transformative manner.

You Are Not Alone

Throughout this exploration, an underlying theme has been the interconnectedness of all life forms, both terrestrial and extraterrestrial. One of the most empowering recognitions you can have is that you are not alone. Even if you are surrounded by those who do not understand or acknowledge this greater cosmic reality, know that you are part of an expansive and diverse Galactic Family. This includes not only Pleiadians but other Starseeds, Lightworkers, Wayshowers, and spiritually advanced beings across dimensions and universes. Many are working toward similar goals of enlightenment, ascension, and the upliftment of consciousness. You are one among many, yet your individual role is vital. Your unique blend of skills, emotions, and spiritual attributes is your contribution to this grand cosmic tapestry.

Applying What You've Learned

This handbook has been layered with concepts, practical tips, and philosophical underpinnings that range from Pleiadian social structures to advanced energy manipulation techniques. The importance of applying these teachings cannot be understated. Theory and knowledge become potent only when put into practice. Whether you focus on healing modalities, deepen your understanding of Pleiadian ethics, or venture into building terrestrial communities that reflect galactic values, the real magic happens in the doing. Don't allow this book to become a relic on your shelf. Make it a living document that you revisit and employ as a resource in your daily life. Theoretical understanding is just the scaffold; the edifice is built by daily practice, community interactions, and continued learning.

Your Cosmic Voyage is Unceasing

Your journey as a Pleiadian Starseed or spiritual seeker is not limited to your time on Earth or even to this current lifetime. Your soul's voyage is a multi-dimensional, eternal adventure. As you awaken more fully to your higher self, and as Earth moves closer to collective ascension, your mission will continually evolve. You will unlock new layers of your own being, discover further depths in others, and perhaps even interface more directly with higher-dimensional entities from the Pleiades or beyond. Though the roadmap presented in this book is extensive, it's crucial to remember that maps can be updated, that the road itself is ever-changing, and sometimes, the most transformative paths are the detours that were never anticipated.

This book was designed to be both a beginning and a reference —a starting point and a periodic touchstone as you navigate the unfolding landscapes of your own cosmic mission. As you turn this page and move forward, consider this not as a conclusion but as a harmonious pause, a moment to integrate before you launch into your next cycle of growth, exploration, and cosmic contribution. You are a critical part of this vast and beautiful universe, and your journey is far from over. Thank you for allowing this handbook to be a part of your adventure. May your path be filled with light, wisdom, and an ever-deepening connection to your Galactic Family.

THE END

Made in the USA
Columbia, SC
24 February 2025